THE
QPR
MISCELLANY

ASH ROSE

First published 2012

The History Press
The Mill, Brimscombe Port
Stroud, Gloucestershire, GL5 2QG
www.thehistorypress.co.uk

British Library Cataloguing in Publication Data.
A catalogue record for this book is available from the British Library.

ISBN 978 0 7524 6738 2

Typesetting and origination by The History Press
Printed in Great Britain
Manufacturing managed by Jellyfish Print Solutions Ltd

FOREWORD

by Kevin Gallen

I've often said that Queens Park Rangers is the 'biggest, smallest club' in English football; it's a special club, a family club where everyone is connected, and it's essentially my club. I was lucky enough to spend fourteen years of my playing career at Loftus Road, spanning three very different eras. And for a boy who was brought up in Shepherd's Bush, to play, score and captain the Rs, I really did live the dream.

When my father first moved to London from Ireland in the late 1960s he landed in Shepherd's Bush and QPR were his local team and therefore became his team, one he still goes to see today as a season ticket holder in the South Africa Road stand. So when my two brothers and I got into football, just like the author of this book, I was taken to Loftus Road and in turn we all became Queens Park Rangers fans. My first game would have to be in about 1979 or 1980, and although I can't recall who we played on that day, I remember growing up in the 1980s watching a fantastic Rangers team – and one that was very much underrated. As good as the 1976 team was (although a little bit before my time), the sides of the 1980s appeared in an FA Cup final, a League Cup final and even qualified for Europe. I grew up watching stars like Terry Fenwick, Simon Stainrod, Gary Waddock under Terry Venables and later Gary Bannister and John Byrne – players that were really underrated and ones you'll see mentioned throughout the book.

My own QPR career began when I joined the club a schoolboy in 1988, turning down both Watford and Chelsea to join the team I supported, and later signed professional terms with the club on 21 September 1994 – my seventeenth birthday. At the time Rangers were a top-flight side and boasted players such as Ray Wilkins, Les Ferdinand and Alan McDonald, and under a QPR legend such as Gerry Francis, a great, great team and who for me personally I was in awe of. Having done well for the youth team, I travelled with the first-team squad for the last game of the 1993/94 season and was promoted to the squad for the start of the following season, making my debut at, of all places, Old Trafford on the first day of the campaign. Although we lost the game 2–0, I thought I played well and even had a goal disallowed – something which I still remind the ref that day (Dermot Gallagher) of to this day. From that moment I was lucky enough to play in over 400 games for Rangers and experience three different periods in Rangers history; the last Premier League heyday, the frustrating decline in the late 1990s and the renaissance of the club under Ian Holloway. That team under Holloway was perhaps the happiest time of my Rangers career, as we won promotion to the Championship with a team of great pros and great personalities that had such a bond and one that I was honoured to be captain of. The goal at Hillsborough in 2004 that secured our promotion will go down as one of my favourite QPR goals, along with my strike against Chelsea in 1994 that later spurred the fans' song about me that I'm so proud to hear every time they sing it.

My career at Rangers ended in 2007, having scored 97 goals for the club with my only regret being that I never quite nabbed a century of goals. But for a local lad to wear the blue and white hoops for so long, and enjoy so many good times for my club I feel incredibly fortunate.

Enjoy the book, it includes some great stories, memorable profiles and facts that I wasn't even aware of about a truly special club.

C'MON YOU RRRRRs!

Kevin Gallen, 2012
(QPR 1994–2000 & 2001–7)

WHEN TWO BECAME ONE

The origins of Queens Park Rangers Football Club began in 1882, on a newly built residential estate in West London, and the formation of two local youth club teams – St Jude's Institute and Christchurch Rangers. St Jude's was set up by local scholars Jack McDonald and Fred Weller for boys of the Droop Street Board School and supported by the Revd Gordon Young, while Christchurch Rangers were formed by footballer George Wodehouse Senior. In 1886, a friend suggested to Wodehouse, who had recently played in a match between the two boys' sides, that a merger would benefit both clubs and a decision was made to form one football club. However, when the newly combined team played under the name of St Jude's Institute and used the Institute as its headquarters, many of the Christchurch players claimed they had been victims of a takeover and they walked out angrily. Their response was to set up a rival club called Paddington FC.

It was important that the few remaining members of Christchurch Rangers should feel fully included in the union and to achieve this, a new name acceptable to everyone had to be found. The name Queens Park Rangers was then chosen for the new club, a name suggested by an E.D. Robertson because the teams and majority of the players were based on the Queen's Park estate of West London. Little did these gentlemen know that this amalgamation would produce a football club that would still be going 125 years later. To celebrate this, a plaque was unveiled at St Jude's town hall in July 2011 marking the 125th anniversary of the team's merger. And QPR also celebrated the milestone on their 2011/12 home shirt, with a '125' motif sewn into the back of the collar.

The earliest details of a Queens Park Rangers game are from a first-team friendly in November 1888 that saw Rangers, wearing contrasting blue-halved shirts, beat Harlesden United 4–1. Two years later QPR competed in their first ever competitive match when they played Tottenham Hotspur in the second round of the London Senior Cup. The game finished

5

1–1 before Rangers lost the replay a week later. Eight years on, in 1898 a decision was made for QPR to become a professional club, and joined the Southern League for the 1899/90 season. In 1920 they finally joined the Football League in the newly formed Third Division.

AROUND THE GROUNDS

QPR hold the title of having had the most home grounds in Football League history, having played in sixteen different locations since their formation.

Welford's Dairy, 1886–7
Rangers played their games at Welford's Dairy; on a ground behind the Case is Altered public house in Kensal Rise up to 1887.

London Scottish Ground, 1888–89
They moved to the London Scottish Ground, Brondesbury, in 1888 and stayed there for one season for an annual rent of £20.

Home Farm, 1891
In 1891 the club was on the move again this time to Home Farm located at Kensal Green.

Kilburn Cricket Club, 1892
A year later Rangers spent a season at the Kilburn Cricket Club in Harvest Road.

Gun Club, 1893
Situated in Wood Lane, QPR's next ground in 1893 was the Gun Club at Wormwood Scrubs.

Kensal Rise Athletic Ground, 1896

1896 saw Rangers take out a 10-year lease on the Kensal Rise Athletic Ground.

Latimer Road, 1901–4

QPR moved to Latimer Road near St Quintin Avenue in 1901. The ground played host to the open-air coronation celebration for King Edward VII, leaving the pitch in a poor condition for the majority of the club's stay.

Agricultural Showground, Park Royal, 1904–7

The 40,000 horse-ring enclosure at the Agricultural Showground became Rangers' next ground in 1904. The area had a large grandstand on one side and a smaller one on the south and was their home for three years.

Park Royal Stadium, 1907–17

Half a mile from the Agricultural Showground, the brand new Park Royal Stadium built by the Great Western Railway Company hosted Rs games from 1907 until 1917.

White City, 1912

This was used as a temporary home in 1912 owing to rail strikes.

Loftus Road, 1917–31

Due to Park Royal being turned into allotments during the First World War, Rangers were seeking a new home in 1917 and relocated to the ground of disbanded club Shepherd's Bush FC in Ellerslie. They re-erected an old stand from Park Royal and altered it to include dressing rooms and an office. It became known as Loftus Road, the name of the road that ran along the eastern edge of the ground.

Highbury, 1930

Owing to crowd trouble the FA closed Loftus Road for two weeks, forcing Rangers to temporarily play home games at Highbury, North London.

White City Stadium, 1931–32

In 1931 Rangers moved to 60,000-capacity stadium White City while keeping Loftus Road as a stage for reserve matches.

Loftus Road, 1933–62

Two years later QPR returned to Loftus Road as the club were losing money, having failed to fill out White City stadium and making a loss of over £34,000.

White City Stadium, 1962–63

1962 saw a second attempt to relocate to White City to increase revenue.

Loftus Road, 1963–present

The move only lasted one season and Rangers moved to the final permanent home back at Loftus Road in 1963.

Highbury, 1984

Rangers were forced to play a 1984 UEFA Cup tie at Highbury due to European Club competition rules preventing games on plastic pitches.

ROLL OF HONOUR

Division One runners-up	1975/76
Division Two/Championship winners	1982/83, 2010/11
Division Two runners-up	1967/68, 1972/73, 2003/04
Division Two play-off finalists	2002/03
Division Three winners	1966/67

Division Three South winners	1947/48
Division Three South runners-up	1946/47
Division Three (Regional) winners	1945/46
Southern League winners	1907/08, 1911/12
Western League winners	1905/06
FA Cup runners-up	1981/82
League Cup winners	1966/67
League Cup runners-up	1985/86
FA Charity Shield runners-up	1908/09, 1911/12
Southern Charity Cup winners	1912/13
West London Challenge Cup finalists	1890/91
West London Observer Cup winners	1892/93
West London Observer Cup runners-up	1893/94

UNITED NATIONS

Since Nigerian-born Tesi Balogun became the first player from outside the UK and Ireland to appear for Rangers, players from all over the world have plied their trade at Loftus Road. Here is a run-down of Rangers' foreign legion and the countries they were born in.

Argentina – Osvaldo Ardiles (1988–9), Gino Padula (2002–5), Emmanuel Ledesma (2008–9), Alejandro Faurlin (2009–)

Australia – Ned Zelic (1995–6), Andrew McDermott (1996–7), Richard Johnson (2004), Nicky Ward (2006–7)

Barbados – Gregory Goodridge (1995–6)

Belgium – Michel Ngonge (2000–1)

Cameroon – Armel Tchakounte (2005–6)

Canada – Paul Peschisolido (2000)

Congo – Serge Branco (2004–5), Pat Kanyuka (2005–8)

Czech Republic – Jan Stejskal (1990–4), Ludek Miklosko (1998–2001), Radek Cerny (2009–)

Denmark – Kurt Bakholt (1986), Mikkel Beck (2000), Marc Nygaard (2005–8), Sammy Youssouf (2006)

Finland – Antti Heinola (1998–2001), Sampsa Timoska (2007–8)

France – Aziz Ben Askar (2001–2), Alex Bonnot (2001–2), George Santos (2004–6), Eric Sabin (2003–4), Pascal Chimbonda (2011), Armand Traore (2011–)

Germany – Steve Lomas (2005–7)

Ghana – Junior Agogo (2002)

Greece – Georgios Tofas (2011)

Holland – Sieb Dykstra (1994–6)

Hungary – George Kulcsar (1997–2001), Akos Buzsaky (2007–), Tamas Priskin (2010)

Iceland – Heidar Helguson (2008–)

Israel – David Pizanti (1987), Ben Sahar (2007)

Italy – Mauro Milanese (2005–7), Generoso Rossi (2005), Matteo Alberti (2008–11), Damiano Tommasi (2008–9), Samuel Di Carmine (2009–10), Alessandro Pellicori (2009–11)

Ivory Coast – Arthur Gnohere (2004–5)

Jamaica – Bob Hazell (1979–83), Damion Stewart (2006–10)

Latvia – Kaspars Gorkss (2008–11)

Malta – Joe Cini (1959–60)

Morocco – Adel Taarabt (2009–)

Nigeria – Tesi Balogun (1956–7), Dominic Iofa (1990–1), Ademola Bankole (1999–2001), Danny Shittu (2001–6, 2011–), Ugo Ukah (2005–6), Egutu Oliseh (2006–7)

Norway – Petter Vaagan Moen (2011–)

Poland – Adam Czerkas (2006–7), Marcin Kus (2006)

Portugal – Bruno Andrade (2010–)

Serbia – Dusko Tosic (2010)

Spain – Inigo Idiakez (2007), Daniel Parejo (2008), Jordi Lopez (2009)

South Africa – Mark Stein (1988–9), Roy Wegerle (1989–92)

Suriname – Sammy Koejoe (1999–2001)

Sweden – Rob Steiner (1988–9)

USA – Juergen Sommer (1995–8), Frankie Simek (2004)

Venezuela – Fernando De Ornelas (2001)

Zaire – Doudou (2001)

TRUE COLOURS

The blue and white hooped kit of Queens Park Rangers is one of the most distinctive jerseys in English football, but they haven't always played in those familiar colours. Upon their formation in the 1880s the team wore an Oxford and Cambridge blue halved shirt, with white shorts and navy blue socks. In 1892, when the club began taking part in competitive football, they played in hoops for the first time, but green and white hoops, colours more traditionally associated with Scottish side Celtic. They wore this strip until 1927, but seeking a change in fortune on the pitch the club decided to change the green hoops for blue ones. The change worked as QPR finished in the top half of the league for the next four successive seasons – their most consistent spell since joining the league in 1920.

After winning promotion to Division Two in 1948, Rangers played in an unfamiliar blue version of the Arsenal shirt before reverting back to the blue and white hoops the following campaign, adding hooped socks to the strip for the first time. A spell back in Division Three South between 1952 and 1958 saw Rangers once again drop the hoops in favour of an all-white shirt and blue shorts until finally adopting the hoops for good in 1960. The blue and white hoops have gone through their own changes over the years too, with red being added to each hoop in the 1980s and 2010s, and even a fluorescent yellow piping appearing in the early 1990s. For the 2011/12 season, Rangers can be seen in a simpler shirt with a greater number of hoops then in recent seasons.

Away from home, Rangers have traditionally favoured a black and red variation of the home shirt, often dubbed the 'Dennis The Menace' shirt – a term Rangers used to their advantage in 2007, when they teamed up with the long-running comic to launch that season's new away jersey with a promotion at the club shop that included characters from the *Beano* wearing the new shirt.

Aside from the common black and red, the away jersey has taken on many forms including the classic red and white quarters of the 1970s, the garish fluorescent yellow and black number from the early 2000s and the 2011/12 mango orange coloured change kit.

ALL-TIME TOP-FLIGHT TABLE

Combining the top-flight records of all teams who have competed in the First Division and Premier League, at the end of October 2011 QPR are ranked 35th out of 64 teams. Top of the table are Liverpool with 5,133 points, while bottom are Glossop North End with 18 (albeit having only played 34 matches to Liverpool's 3,839). QPR have 981 points from 831 games.

QPR TIMELINE – THE EARLY YEARS

1886 – St Jude's Institute and Christchurch Rangers merged to form Queens Park Rangers Football Club.

1890 – First competitive match, a 1–1 draw with Tottenham Hotspur.

1892 – Joined West London League; moved grounds to Kilburn Cricket Club.

1893 – Beat Fulham 3–2 in the West London Observer Cup final to win the club's first piece of silverware.

1895 – Entered FA Cup for the first time, losing in the first round to Old St Stephens.

1896 – Acquired services of Jock Campbell and joined the London League Second Division.

1897 – Elevated to London League First Division along with Bromley and local rivals Brentford.

1898 – First game against opponents outside of London, losing 4–1 to West Bromwich Albion in a friendly.

1899 – Turned professional and joined the Southern League, beat Brighton United 6–0 in their first professional game.

PLASTIC FANTASTIC

In 1981 QPR and manager Terry Venables made the controversial move to have the grass pitch at Loftus Road dug up and replaced with Astroturf, becoming the first English club to play on a 'plastic pitch'. The £350,000 project was seen as a major step forward and a way to make money on the ground, as QPR would be able to rent it out to non-footballing events. However, it was largely condemned by the football community with players constantly finding themselves with burns and sustaining unusual injuries. There were also concerns with the bounce of the ball on the pitch, which would often confuse players and become a nightmare to judge for goalkeepers.

Jim Smith was QPR manager during the Omniturf (as it was the called) era at Loftus Road said of the controversial move, 'It was a nightmare. It was a false game; I knew exactly when we were going to score. It was like robots playing. You got carpet burns and very bad backs if you played on them long enough. The likes of ourselves who played on it regularly had a big advantage.'

Rangers' first game on the plastic pitch came on 1 September 1981, with a 2–1 win ironically over Luton Town, who would later follow Rangers in laying their own plastic pitch along with Oldham Athletic and Preston North End. Ultimately, QPR got used to playing on the surface and it became an advantage over other teams. It was a common sight to see Rangers players in tights and gloves whatever the weather as a way of preventing injuries and coping with the unusual pitch. Rangers played on the plastic pitch for seven seasons until 1988, when the surface was ripped up and replaced with a new grass pitch.

TURKISH DELIGHT

Before the start of the 1948/49 season Rangers became the first British team to make an official trip to play in Turkey. In May 1948, the Rs played in four matches at the 22,000 capacity Istanbul Stadium, only losing once to the Turkish Olympic side by two goals to one.

QPR TIMELINE – 1900 TO 1920s

1900 – Rangers played their first season in the Western League in addition to their Southern League commitments.

1905 – Neil Murphy becomes the first QPR player to win an international cap when he is picked for Ireland.

1906 – QPR become Western League champions.

1907 – Runners-up in the Western League Division 1A.

1908 – Rangers won the Southern League championship but were refused entry into Football League with Tottenham being elected instead. Also, Evelyn Lintott became the first QPR player to be selected to play for England and Rangers compete in the first ever Charity Shield against Manchester United.

1909 – Runners-up in the Western League Division 1A.

1912 – Rangers won the Southern League championship for the second time.

1917 – QPR moved to Loftus Road.

1920 – Became founding members of the Football League, forming the Third Division.

1921 – Football League format changed and Rangers included in the new Third Division South.

1926 – Club colours were changed from green and white hoops to blue and white.

BRAINIAC

In January 2002, QPR Defender Clarke Carlisle was crowned 'Britain's Brainiest Footballer' in an ITV show hosted by Carol Vorderman. The defender, who would later go on to also appear on *Countdown* while a Burnley player, saw off a panel of twelve footballing personalities, including England's World Cup-winning full-back George Cohen and Newcastle striker Malcolm MacDonald. Carlisle, who made 112 appearances for Rangers during a four-year spell, beat former QPR midfielder Alan Brazil 6–5 in the final.

FIVE GREAT GAMES

Fulham 2–3 QPR
22 April 1893, West London Observer
Football Challenge Cup final
The two well-known West London teams met at Kensal Rise in the biggest game so far in both clubs' history, for the West London Observer Football Challenge Cup final. The game kicked-off at 4 p.m. and started at a frantic pace with Fulham shading the opening exchanges but failing to break the deadlock thanks to some erratic finishing and sound defending

from Rangers' Herbert Teagle and Robert Rusbrook. The game remained goalless at half time, but then Rangers, sensing they had weathered the storm and playing with the wind in their favour, took the lead through John Collins. Fulham tried to rally but once again could not get through the Rangers rearguard, and QPR doubled their lead midway through the second half sending the fans into raptures. The game looked as good as won but once again Fulham refused to buckle and forced a way back into the game through Withington before a free kick just 13 minutes from time saw Fulham draw the game level. Both teams strove hard for a winner, but when the referee blew for full time (some 7 minutes earlier than he should have), he ordered an extra half-hour to be played to find a winner.

The game became fast and frantic with both sides laying siege to their opponents' goal, looking to settle the tie. QPR's Albert Morris then tried a shot that May fisted out, only for Morris to return the ball and with May falling, the ball bounced into the net to give QPR the upper hand with the last quarter of an hour to play. Fulham tried to retrieve the game but ultimately could not force an equaliser and Rangers held on for a famous victory and their first piece of silverware.

QPR team: Craber, Rushbrook, Teagle, McKenzie, Harvey, Maund, Wallington, Ward, Davies, Morris, Collins

QPR 6–0 Brighton United
2 September 1899, Southern League
Over 5,000 fans packed into the Kensal Rise ground on 2 September 1899 to witness QPR's first ever professional game against Brighton United in the Southern League. On a rainy afternoon in West London, Rangers started brightly and were two goals to the good inside 20 minutes, first through Frank Bedingfield, who went into the record books as the scorer of QPR's first ever professional goal, and then Andrew Cowie. Rangers continued to dominate and further goals through Peter Turnbull and Cowie's second gave the Rs a 4–0 lead at the break. The second half saw Rangers and particularly Cowie

continue to punish the Brighton defence with the Rangers striker netting 2 more goals as QPR ran out 6 goals to the good. It proved to be the start of a season of stability for Rangers as they ended their first professional season in eighth place in the Southern League, while Brighton United sadly didn't last the season, resigning from the league before the campaign ended.

QPR team: Clutterbuck, Knowles, McConnell, Crawford, Tennant, Keech, Smith, Hayward, Bedingfield, Turnbull, Cowie

QPR 9–2 Tranmere Rovers
3 December 1960, Division Three
QPR went goal crazy and posted their record victory during a Third Division match at Shepherd's Bush in December 1960. Rangers were in angry mood having been dumped out the FA Cup a week earlier and took the lead after 23 minutes through Bernie Evans. By half time further goals from Brian Bedford, Clive Clark and Mark Lazarus put Rangers into a commanding lead and the onslaught continued into the second half. Lazarus added his second, Clark his third before further goals from Evans, Bedford and Jimmy Andrews saw the Super Hoops hit Rovers with a 9-goal blitz. Unfortunately the result was seen in front of QPR's lowest crowd of the season as only 4,805 fans braved the wind and rain to pay witness to a record moment in the club's history.

QPR team: Drinkwater, Woods, Ingham, Keen, Rutter, Angell, Lazarus, Bedford, Evans, Andrews, Clark

QPR 3–2 West Bromwich Albion
4 March 1967, League Cup final
Third Division meets First, 2–0 down to 3–2 up, Rodney Marsh's Wembley wonder. They're all elements etched into Rangers folklore and moments of which make this day the greatest in the club's illustrious history. Wembley hosted its first ever League Cup final as underdogs Queens Park Rangers took on top-flight favourites West Bromwich Albion. By half

time the game was going true to form with the Baggies cruising to a 2–0 lead and Rangers looked down and out. However, a second half dominated by QPR eventually saw Alec Stock's men force their way back into the game thanks to a Roger Morgan header, then minutes later Marsh produced his bit of magic to level the game. With 8 minutes left on the clock it was the team in all white in the ascendency and they were rewarded when Mark Lazarus was first to a loose ball in the box and netted the Rs' most famous goal and their only major trophy.

QPR team: Springett, Hazell, Langley, Keen, Hunt, Sibley, Lazarus, Sanderson, Allen, Marsh, Morgan

QPR 4–0 Brann Bergen
15 September 1976, UEFA Cup first round
QPR's second-place finish in 1976 meant that for the first time in their history they would compete in Europe the following season. In the first round of the UEFA Cup Rangers were drawn against Norwegian side Brann Bergen and on 15 September 1976 played their first ever European game at Loftus Road. The game was a great advert for European football with both teams playing some attractive free-flowing play, but it was Rangers who took the lead on the half-hour through maverick Stan Bowles, getting on the end of David Webb's flick. Four minutes later Bowles made it 2 and completed a famous hat-trick midway through the second half. Don Masson added a fourth with 5 minutes left on the clock as Rangers announced their arrival on the European stage in real style.

QPR team: Parkes, Clement, Gillard, Hollins, McLintock, Webb, Thomas, Leach, Masson, Bowles, Givens

DOUBLE BUBBLE

Dave Clement, arguably Rangers' greatest ever right-back, played for the club twice in same day on 21 May 1960. He spent the afternoon at centre-back playing in the Southern Counties League match against Watford and at right-back that same evening as QPR met the Hornets once again in the Football Combination League. That's dedication.

LOFTUS ROAD LEGEND – GEORGE GODDARD

Having made his name at amateur level, George Goddard joined Queens Park Rangers from Redhill in March 1926. The striker made his debut wearing the number 9 shirt the following September, scoring in the 4–2 defeat to Brentford and went on to score 23 goals in 38 games that season. He netted a further 26 times in the following campaign before hitting his peak over the next 2 years, scoring 38 and 39 goals and passing the 100-goal milestone in just under 3½ years with the club.

Goddard continued to rack up the goals for QPR over the next 3 years and went on to score an incredible 186 goals for Rangers, a haul that remains a club record to this day. In December 1933, Goddard was sold to local rivals Brentford as Rangers tried to raise cash after a spell at White City Stadium had put strain on the clubs finances. After Brentford, Goddard had spells with Wolverhampton Wanderers, Sunderland and Southend United before retiring from football to run a confectionery and tobacco shop in Moseley, West Midlands, until his death in March 1987.

DID YOU KNOW?

When Rangers signed George Goddard he was working part-time at a local bus company.

BIGGER THAN JESUS

In a 1998 internet poll, former Manchester City defender Jamie Pollock was voted number one by QPR fans in a vote to find the most influential man of the past 2,000 years, despite never having played for the club. The vote was down to Pollock's infamous own goal during a match between City and Rangers that year that saw the Rs preserve their First Division status ahead of the Manchester club. Pollock found himself ahead of a whole of host of famous names including Jesus, who was second.

CHARITY FIRST

Queens Park Rangers competed in the first ever Charity Shield match against Manchester United on 27 April 1908. The competition had been preceded by the Sheriff of London Charity Shield that pitted the best professional and amateur teams against each other, but the format evolved at the end of the 1907/08 season when Football League winners United took on Southern League champions QPR. The game was played at Stamford Bridge in front of 12,000 fans and it was, at the time, Rangers' biggest game in their history so far. The United team included many household names of the era, including Welsh star Billy Meredith, but it was Rangers who took lead through Fred Cannon. They held the advantage until late in the game when Meredith equalised and forced the game to a replay. The replay, played some 4 months later in the August as a curtain-raiser to the new season, was again held at Stamford Bridge and ended in a convincing 4–0 win for a strong United side. After the match both sides went to the Alhambra Theatre in London where they watched a bioscope replay of the game together. Rangers' share of the gate was £100, which they donated to charities – St Mary's Hospital (£50), Willesden College Hospital (£25), Acton College Hospital (£15) and Willesden Children's Aid (£10). The game remains the only Charity Shield or Community Shield match to ever go to a replay.

27 April 1908
Manchester United 1–1 QPR (Meredith, Cannon)
Manchester United: Moger, Stacey, Burgess, Duckworth, Roberts, Bell, Meredith, Bannister, Turnbull, Turnbull, Wall.

Queens Park Rangers: Shaw, MacDonald, Fidler, Lintott, McLean, Downing, Pentland, Cannon, Skilton, Gittins, Barnes.

Replay
29 August 1908
Manchester United 4–0 QPR (Turnbull 3, Wall)

Manchester United: Moger, Stacey, Burgess, Duckworth, Roberts, Bell, Meredith, Bannister, Turnbull, Picken, Wall.

Queens Park Rangers: Shaw, MacDonald, Fidler, Lintott, McLean, Downing, McNaught, Cannon, Skilton, Gittins, Barnes.

NUMBERS GAME

To capitalise on the growing monopoly of the Premier League, squad numbers were introduced into English football for the first time in 1993, giving each member of a first-team squad their own name and number on the back of their shirt. Six years later, the Football League followed suit and they have since become a common sight in modern-day football. The following is a complete history of who has worn what squad number at QPR since their introduction.

1
Tony Roberts, Ludek Miklosko, Chis Day, Simon Royce, Lee Camp, Paddy Kenny

2
David Bardsley, Tim Breacker, Mark Perry, Terrell Forbes, Marcus Bignot, Damien Delaney, Peter Ramage, Bradley Orr

3

Clive Wilson, Rufus Brevett, Ian Baraclough, Paul Bruce, Gino Padula, Mauro Milanese, Chris Barker, Damion Stewart, Clint Hill

4

Ray Wilkins, Steve Yates, Simon Barker, Steve Morrow, Steve Palmer, Richard Edghill, Ian Evatt, Danny Cullip, Gavin Mahon, Shaun Derry

5

Darren Peacock, Karl Ready, Alan McDonald, Clarke Carlisle, Danny Shittu, Zesh Rehman, Damion Stewart, Fitz Hall

6

Alan McDonald, Danny Maddix, Chris Plummer, Danny Shittu, Richard Johnson, Andrew Davies, Tommy Doherty, Michael Mancienne, Mikele Leigertwood, Danny Gabbidon

7

Andy Impey, Paul Murray, Stuart Wardley, Matthew Rose, Adam Bolder, Daniel Parejo, Wayne Routledge, Marcus Bent, Adel Taarabt

8

Ian Holloway, Gavin Peacock, Marc Bircham, Daniel Nardiello, Rowan Vine, Leon Clarke, Kieron Dyer

9

Les Ferdinand, Daniele Dichio, Rob Steiner, Michel Ngonge, Richard Langley, Tony Thorpe, Dean Sturridge, Nick Ward, Dexter Blackstock, Heidar Helguson, DJ Campbell

10

Bradley Allen, Kevin Gallen, Karl Connolly, Akos Buzsaky, Jay Bothroyd

11

Trevor Sinclair, Chris Kiwomya, Marcus Bignot, Karl Connolly, Gareth Ainsworth, Patrick Agyemang, Alejandro Faurlin

12

Gary Penrice, Paul Murray, Matthew Rose, Doudou, Eric Sabin, Marcus Bignot, Nick Culkin, Jake Cole, Adam Bolder, Alessandro Pellicori, Jamie Mackie

13

Jan Stejskal, Sieb Dykstra, Lee Harper, Nikki Bull, Nick Culkin, Jake Cole, Kaspars Gorkss, Armand Traore

14

Simon Barker, Karl Ready, Antti Heinola, Leon Knight, Leroy Griffiths, Chris Plummer, Martin Rowlands, Akos Buzsaky

15

Rufus Brevett, George Kulcsar, Christer Warren, Gavin Peacock, Steve Lovell, Simon Royce, Lee Cook, Kevin McLeod, Richard Pacquette, Jamie Cureton, George Santos, Dominic Shimmin, Peter Ramage, Ben Watson, Nigel Quashie, Kyle Walker, Wayne Routledge, Bruno Perone

16

Danny Maddix, Keith Rowland, Hamid Barr, Danny Murphy, Wes Daly, Marcus Bean, Sammy Youssef, Steve Lomas, Ray Jones, Jason Jarrett, Matt Connelly

17

Dennis Bailey, Chris Plummer, Terrell Forbes, Lyndon Duncan, Marcus Bean, Lee Cook, Ben Sahar, Patrick Agyemang, Lee Cook, Joey Barton

18

Karl Ready, Alan McCarthy, Gregory Goodridge, Steve Slade, Clarke Carlisle, Sammy Koejoe, Robert Taylor, Dominic Foley, Kevin Gallen, Oliver Burgess, Dennis Oli, Kevin McLeod, Stefan Bailey, Stephen Moore, Armel Tchakounte, Matt Pickens, Damiano Tomassi, Liam Miller, Alejandro Faurlin, Gavin Mahon, Luke Young

19

Devon White, Nigel Quashie, Ademola Bankole, Christer Warren, Dave McEwen, Marcus Bean, Brian Fitzgerald, Ben Walshe, Terrell Forbes, Serge Branco, Generoso Rossi, Aaron Brown, Marcin Kus, Simon Walton, Angelo Balanta, Patrick Agyemang

20

Maurice Doyle, Kevin Gallen, Ray Wilkins, Tony Scully, Lyndon Duncan, Dennis Oli, Warren Barton, Arthur Gnohere, Wes Daly, Dean Sturridge, Dominic Shimmin, Scott Donnelly, Lee Camp, Kieron St Aimie, Emmanuel Ledesma, Jorgi López, Tommy Williams, Rob Hulse

21

Tony Witter, Steve Yates, Richard Langley, Justin Cochrane, Wes Daly, Marien Ifura, Jack Perry, Adam Miller, Phil Barnes, Paul Jones, John Curtis, Kieran Lee, Matteo Alberti, Tommy Smith

22

Michael Meaker, Lee Charles, Jermaine Darlington, Richard Pacquette, Marcus Bean, Kevin McLeod, Arthur Gnohere, Matthew Hislop, Shabazz Baidoo, Samuel Di Carmine, Tom Heaton, Rhys Taylor, Carl Ikeme, Peter Ramage, Heidar Helguson

23

Peter Caldwell, Andy McDermott, Leon Jeanne, Marcus Bignot, Danny Murphy, Leroy Griffiths, Richard Edghill, George Santos, Stefan Bailey, Jake Cole, Jay Simpson, Petter Vaagan Moen

24

Steve Yates, Daniele Dichio, Trevor Challis, Mark Perry, Oliver Burgess, Richard Pacquette, Jake Cole, Pat Kanyuka, Radek Cerny

25

Alan McCarthy, Steve Hodge, Juergen Sommer, Iain Dowie, Alex Higgins, Ben Walshe, Patrick Gradley, Jonathan Fletcher, Scott Donnelly, Luke Townsend, Damion Stewart, Bob Malcolm, Hogan Ephraim

26

Ray Wilkins, Mark Hateley, Richard Graham, Alex Bonnot, Jerome Thomas, Ben Walshe, Ryan Johnson, Rowan Vine, Gareth Ainsworth, Dusko Tosic, Gary Borrowdale

27

Maurice Doyle, Matthew Brazier, Stuart Wardley, Andy Thomson, Dean Marney, Aaron Brown, Scott Donnelly, Adam Czerkas, Sampsa Timoska, Heidar Helguson, Lee Brown, Peter Ramage

28

Chris Plummer, Darren Currie, Peter Crouch, Aziz Ben Askar, David Wattley, Jamie Cureton, Leon Best, Frankie Simek, Dominic Shimmin, Shabazz Baidoo, Egutu Oliseh, Inigo Indiakez, Zesh Rehman, Joe Ostler, Danny Shittu

29

Ross Weare, Doudou, Paul Furlong, Nicky Ward, Fitz Hall, Gary Borrowdale, Ismael Miller, Danny Shittu, Michael Doughty

30

Paul Bruce, Fraser Digby, Richard Johnson, Luke Mulholland, Marc Nygaard, Romone Rose, Troy Hewitt

31

Sammy Koejoe, Danny Shittu, Brett Angell, Luke Townsend, Steve Lomas, Ray Jones

32

Darren Ward, Danny Grieves, Fernando de Ornelas, Patrick Gradley, Jerome Thomas, Stephen Kelly, Simon Royce, Ugo

Ukah, Dexter Blackstock, Mikele Leigertwood, Antonio German, Elvis Putnins, Shaun Wright-Phillips

33
Terry McFlynn, Aaron Brown, Paul Furlong, Rhys Evans, Tommy Williams, Matthew Hislop, Lloyd Dyer, Andy Taylor, Jonathan Munday, Andrew Howell, Martin Crainie, Reece Crowther, Antonio German

34
Nikki Bull, Carl Leaburn, Dominic Foley, Callum Willock, Shabazz Baidoo, Andrew Howell, Matthew Hislop, Rohan Ricketts, Scott Sinclair, Niki-Lee Bulmer, Ed Harris, Max Ehmer

35
Chris Goodchild, Josh Parker, Anton Ferdinand

36
Mikkel Beck, Marlon Broomes, Dennis Oli, Danny Murphy, Leon Clarke, Ray Jones, Angelo Balanta, Steven Reid, Tamas Priskin, Bruno Andrade

37
Gareth Taylor, Paul Peschisolido, Ben Walshe, Keith Lowe, Jimmy Smith, Romone Rose, Shane McWeeney, Georgios Tofas, Lee Cook

38
Richard Pacquette, Kevin Lisbie, Junior Agogo, Michael Mancienne, Michael Doughty, Martin Rowlands

39
Ben Walshe, Kieron St Aimie, Adel Taarabt, Pascal Chimbonda, Jordan Gibbons

40
Justin Cochrane, Richard Langley, Ugo Ukah, Michael Harriman

41
Danny Shittu

42
Troy Hewitt, Antonio German, Jason Puncheon

QPR TIMELINE – 1930s & 1940s

1931 – Club relocated to White City Stadium.

1932 – A record home gate of 41,097 established as QPR beat Leeds on 9 January in the FA Cup third round.

1933 – Rangers returned to Loftus Road.

1935 – The first QPR Supporters' Club was formed.

1939 – Football League programme suspended due to the outbreak of the Second World War. Rangers spent the war years competing in specially formed South (B) League.

1945 – Cyril Hatton became Rangers' first £1,000 signing, joining from Notts County.

1946 – Football League Division Three South runners-up.

1948 – Rangers are promoted for the first time, winning the Third Division South.

LOFTUS ROAD LEGEND – TONY INGHAM

Yorkshire-born defender Ingham signed from Leeds United for a fee of £5,000 in June 1950. He made only three starts in three years while at Elland Road, though he slotted straight into the

Rangers team making his debut in a 2–1 defeat to Doncaster Rovers in November of that year and going to make 23 starts during his first season at Loftus Road. He added a further 18 appearances in the Rangers side before making the left-back spot his own at the start of the 1951/52 season, playing 46 times that season and scoring his first ever goal for the club in a 4–2 loss to Crystal Palace.

Ingham became an integral member of the first team throughout the mid-1950s and from February 1955 to September 1961, he didn't miss a single game – an incredible run of 250 consecutive appearances. Ingham retired from football in 1963, playing his last game for the Rs in May 1963 against Coventry City aged 38, having made a club record of 555 appearances in all competitions.

Tony remained close with the club after his retirement, becoming Commercial Director in 1981 and staying on the club board until the early 1990s. He sadly passed away in April 2010.

DID YOU KNOW?

Before his time at QPR, Tony Ingham served in the Royal Navy during the Second World War and also completed an electrical apprenticeship.

SAY WHAT, OLLIE?

As manager of Queens Park Rangers between 2001 and 2006, Ian Holloway became one the most successful and popular managers in the club's history, leading them to promotion in 2004. Equally he became infamous for his pre- and post-match interviews, where his unique way with words mixed with his distinctive Bristolian accent spawned quotes that would affectionately become known as 'Ollieisms'.

'Most of our fans get behind us and are fantastic, but those who don't should shut the hell up or they can come round my house and I will fight them.'

After a troubling day at QPR

'I can't see into the future. Last year I thought I was going to Cornwall on my holidays but I ended up going to Lyme Regis.'

On whether QPR could beat Man City

'To put it in gentleman's terms if you've been out for a night and you're looking for a young lady and you pull one, some weeks they're good looking and some weeks they're not the best. Our performance today would have been not the best looking bird but at least we got her in the taxi. She wasn't the best looking lady we ended up taking home but she was very pleasant and very nice, so thanks very much, let's have a coffee.'

Describing an 'ugly' win for QPR at Chesterfield

'Paul Furlong is my vintage Rolls-Royce and he cost me nothing. We polish him, look after him, and I have him fine-tuned by my mechanics. We take good care of him because we have to drive him every day, not just save him for weddings.'

On Paul Furlong, his veteran striker at QPR

'Anybody who is a QPR fan is welcome at Loftus Road. I'd be happy for him to turn up for a kickabout, just so long as he brings that Kate Moss with him – she's absolutely lovely.'

On QPR fan Pete Doherty

'Right now, everything is going wrong for me – if I fell in a barrel of boobs, I'd come out sucking my thumb.'

On a tricky run of results

'Well some of them might get their hair done.'

On whether being on TV may affect his team

'When you play with wingers you look like a taxi with both doors open. Anyone can get in or out.'

On a poor pre-season performance

'In football there is no definite lifespan or timespan for a manager. After a while you start smelling of fish. The other week it looked like I was stinking of halibut.'

On a bad start to the season

'He's a big lad. He can clean out your guttering without standing on a ladder.'

On George Santos

'The games are coming thick and fast for him. I've told him to go down to Iceland and ask if he can sit on one of their freezers.'

On Danny Shittu returning from injury

'Everyone calls him a Gypsy, but I can assure you he does not live in a caravan. He has a house with foundations.'

On Gino Padula's and the away fans

'It's like that film *Men In Black*. I walk around in a black suit, white shirt and black tie where I've had to flash my white light every now and then to erase some memories.'

On QPR's financial situation

'It's all very well having a great pianist, but it's no good if you haven't got anyone to get the piano on the stage in the first place. Otherwise the pianist would be standing there with no bloody piano to play!'

On defensive midfielders

'I used to keep parakeets and I never counted every egg thinking I would get all eight birds. You just hoped they came out of the nest looking all right.'

On developing players

GOTCHA!

Noel's House Party was a staple of Saturday night television during the 1990s and one of the era's most watched shows. Presented by Noel Edmonds, one of the show's most famous regulars was the 'Gotcha Oscar', a segment that involved stitching up celebrities with some elaborate and ultimately humorous set-up before Noel would reveal himself from under a disguise to present the unlucky star with their gong. In 1993, at the height of Rangers' last Premier League heyday, they became the only football club to ever fall victim to one of Noel's mischievous pranks with a staged and ultimately embarrassing new kit launch. The set-up involved dressing up stars including Les Ferdinand and Alan McDonald in newly designed strips that included fur, sequins and even a cape. Needless to say there were a few famous red faces on Noel's sofa the following week when the team honourably collected their 'award'.

THE 24TH MAN

Striker Daniele Dichio made over 100 appearances for QPR in a 6-year stint in the early 1990s. However, it was later in his career that he achieved legendary status at another club, MLS franchise Toronto FC, as the scorer of their first ever goal. The 24th-minute strike against Chicago Fire in May 2007 is now celebrated at home games by a chorus of a Dichio-themed songs sung by fans in the 24th minute of every match.

THE MANAGERS

John Bowman 2 September 1902–30 April 1905
P 102   W 41   D 26   L 35   Win % 40.2

James Cowan 2 September 1906–29 April 1914
P 296   W 128   D 85   L 83   Win % 43.2

James Howie 1 September 1914–30 April 1920
P 236   W 85   D 48   L 103   Win % 36.0

Ned Liddell 28 August 1920–2 May 1925
P 224   W 87   D 52   L 85   Win % 38.8

Bob Hewison 25 August 1925 – 2 May 1931
P 265   W 103   L 56   D 106   Win % 38.9

John Bowman 29 August 1931 – 31 October 1931
P 13   W 1   L 6   D 6   Win % 7.7

Archie Mitchell 7 November 1931 – 6 May 1933
P 80   W 32   D 19   L 29   Win % 40.0

Mick O'Brien 26 August 1933 – 4 May 1935
P 90   W 43   D 16   L 31   Win % 47.8

William Birrell 31 August 1935 – 6 May 1939
P 178   W 82   D 42   L 54   Win % 46.1

Ted Vizard 26 August 1939 – 22 April 1944
P 186   W 95   D 29   L 62   Win % 51.1

Dave Mangnall 29 April 1944 – 3 May 1952
P 356   W 150   D 96   L 110   Win % 42.1

Jack Taylor 23 April 1952 – 27 April 1959
P 341   W 118   D 89   L 134   Win % 34.6

Alec Stock 22 August 1959 – 10 May 1968
P 459   W 220   D 106   L 133   Win % 47.9

Bill Dodgin Jr* 10 August 1968 – 2 November 1968
P 18   W 2   D 5   L 11   Win % 11.1

Tommy Docherty 9 November 1968 – 23 November 1968
P 3   W 1   D 0   L 2   Win % 33.3

Les Allen 7 December 1968 – 2 January 1971
P 99   W 31   D 23   L 45   Win % 31.3

Gordon Jago 9 January 1971 – 8 October 1974
P 180   W 79   D 59   L 42   Win % 43.9

Dave Sexton 12 October 1974 – 23 May 1977
P 142   W 65   D 35   L 42   Win % 45.8

Frank Sibley 20 August 1977 – 2 May 1978
P 50   W 12   D 18   L 20   Win % 24.0

Steve Burtenshaw 19 August 1978 – 28 April 1979
P 43   W 8   D 13   L 22   Win % 18.6

Tommy Docherty 11 May 1979 – 1 November 1980
P 67   W 24   D 21   L 22   Win % 35.8

Terry Venables 8 November 1980 – 15 May 1984
P 175   W 89   D 34   L 52   Win % 50.9

Alan Mullery 25 August 1984 – 4 December 1984
P 26   W 11   D 8   L 7   Win % 42.3

Frank Sibley* 8 December 1984 – 11 May 1985
P 29   W 9   D 6   L 14   Win % 31.0

Jim Smith 17 August 1985 – 3 December 1988
P 169   W 67   D 38   L 64   Win % 39.6

Peter Shreeves* 10 December 1988 – 14 December 1988
P 2   W 1   D 1   L 0   Win % 50.0

Trevor Francis 17 December 1988 – 25 November 1989
P 47   W 14   D 17   L 16   Win % 29.8

Don Howe 2 December 1989 – 11 May 1991
P 76   W 27   D 21   L 28   Win % 35.5

Gerry Francis 18 August 1991 – 5 November 1994
P 161   W 59   D 47   L 55   Win % 36.6

Ray Wilkins 9 November 1994 – 1 September 1996
P 80   W 31   D 13   L 36   Win % 38.8

Frank Sibley* 7 September 1994 – 14 September 1994
P 3   W 1   D 1   L 1   Win % 33.3

Stewart Houston 18 September 1996 – 8 November 1997
P 63   W 25   D 15   L 23   Win % 39.7

*John Hollins November 1997 – December 1997
P 5   W 1   D 2   L 2   Win % 20.0

Ray Harford 12 December 1997 – 26 September 1998
P 40   W 5   D 18   L 17   Win % 12.5

Iain Dowie* 29 September 1998 – 21 October 1998
P 4   W 1   D 0   L 3   Win % 25.0

Gerry Francis 25 October 1998 – 24 February 2001
P 123   W 36   D 42   L 45   Win % 29.3

Ian Holloway 3 March 2001 – 5 February 2006
P 252   W 100   D 71   L 81   Win % 39.7

Gary Waddock 6 February 2006 – 20 September 2006
P 24   W 4   D 8   L 12   Win % 16.7

John Gregory 20 September 2006 – 1 October 2007
P 48   W 13   D 12   L 23   Win % 27.1

Mick Harford* 1 October 2007 – 29 October 2007
P 5   W 2   D 2   L 1   Win % 40.2

Luigi De Canio 29 October 2007 – 4 May 2008
P 35   W 12   D 11   L 12   Win % 34.3

Iain Dowie 9 August 2008 – 24 October 2008
P 15   W 8   D 3   L 4   Win % 53.3

Gareth Ainsworth* 24 October 2008 – 19 November 2008
P 6   W 2   D 1   L 3   Win % 26.9

Paulo Sousa 19 November 2008 – 9 April 2009
P 26   W 7   D 12   L 7   Win % 26.9

Gareth Ainsworth* 9 April 2009 – 3 May 2009
P 5   W 1   D 1   L 3 Win % 20.0

Jim Magilton 3 June 2009 – 9 December 2009
P 24   W 9   D 8   L 7   Win % 37.5

Steve Gallen/Marc Bircham December 2009
P 1   W 0   D 1   L 0

Paul Hart 17 December 2009 – 15 January 2010
P 5   W 1   D2   L2   Win % 20.0

Mick Harford* 15 January 2010 – 1 March 2010
P 7   W 1   D 0   L 6   Win % 14.3

Neil Warnock 1 March 2010 –
P 77   W 33   D 25   L 19   Win % 42.86

*Caretaker

FIVE GREAT GAFFERS

Alec Stock

Perhaps Rangers' greatest ever manager, in a 9-year spell Alec Stock took the club from the Third to the First Division and led them to their finest hour and only major trophy. Appointed in the summer of 1959, he took over a team that had only just escaped relegation to the Fourth Division and had a huge job on his hands to turn the club around. He started off by bringing in Brian Bedford from Bournemouth and then Mark Lazarus and together the pair become one of Rangers' most prolific strike forces. Promotion, however, continued to elude his team, until the 1966/67 season where with Rodney Marsh at the fulcrum, Rangers stormed to the Third Division title. That year also saw QPR defy the odds and reach the League Cup final; 98,000 fans packed into the first Wembley final to see Stock's Third Division side overturn a 2–0 deficit to defeat First Division West Bromwich Albion and claim the club's only major piece of silverware. Things got even better for Rangers a year later, as Stock secured back-to-back promotions and a place in the First Division. His time in West London ended in 1968 when he was controversially sacked amid concerns over his ill health. He later enjoyed successful spells at Fulham and Luton Town before retiring in Yeovil. Stock sadly passed away in 2001.

Dave Sexton

It only took three seasons at the helm at Loftus Road to put Dave Sexton among Rangers' most successful managers. Arriving in the autumn of 1974, Sexton inherited a team that included talented players such as Gerry Francis, Stan Bowles and Dave Thomas and set about finding a way of harnessing this talent and creating a side that could challenge for honours. Adding Don Masson to give the team width and later familiar faces from his time at Chelsea – Dave Webb and John Hollins – to add steel. Sexton put together arguably one of the most entertaining teams ever seen in W12. The side was epitomised by Francis' goal on the opening day of the 1975/76 season, a sweeping passing move that would later be voted goal of the season. That goal proved to be the catalyst for a memorable campaign that saw Rangers record their highest ever finish and go within a whisker of the League Championship – only a last-day defeat to Norwich prevented the Rs from reaching the top-spot, finishing a point behind champions Liverpool. Second place did, however, mean UEFA Cup football and Sexton oversaw a first European campaign for the club that saw them beat Brann Bergen, Bratislava and FC Koln before a quarter-final exit at the hands of AEK Athens. A manager with coaching techniques well ahead of his team, Sexton left Rangers in 1977 to boss Manchester United and went on to twice coach England's U21s.

Terry Venables

As a former midfielder with over 170 appearances, fans welcomed Terry Venables back to the club in October 1980, succeeding Tommy Docherty. Seen as a somewhat surprising move having dropped a division from First Division Crystal Palace, Venables was instrumental as Rangers enjoyed their most successful period of the decade. As a Second Division side, Venables led Rangers to their first and to date only FA Cup final appearance, losing to Spurs after a replay in 1982's showpiece. The following season Rangers, with Clive Allen leading from the front, were promoted back to the top flight as champions, finishing the season 10 points ahead of nearest challengers Wolverhampton Wanderers. Venables' progression continued and saw his team consolidate their First Division status with a fifth-place finish, their highest placing since 1976, and earning a place in the UEFA Cup. Unfortunately for Rangers, Spanish giants Barcelona came calling that summer and 'El Tel' left in May 1984 to go on a glittering managerial career that included silverware at the Nou Camp and later at Spurs before coaching England at the 1996 European Championships.

Ian Holloway

Beyond the madcap quotes and Bristolian banter lies a very good manager in Ian Holloway, and one that QPR fans will forever be thankful to for arguably saving the club from its lowest ebb. After cutting his managerial teeth at hometown club Bristol Rovers, Holloway took over the reins at Loftus Road in February 2001, succeeding Gerry Francis. The club which he'd left as a player after their relegation in 1996 had changed dramatically and he could do very little to stop the club from dropping into the third tier that season. With the club in financial turmoil and a skeleton playing staff, Holloway used his eye for a bargain and motivational spirit to rebuild the club. He consolidated their place in the Second Division in his first full campaign and led them first to play-off heartache the year after and then promotion back to the now-rebranded Championship in 2004. Unearthing players such as Danny Shittu and Gino Padula, and combining them with seasoned pros like Kevin Gallen and the revitalised Paul Furlong, Holloway continued to aid Rangers' revival with a successful first season back in the Championship and an eleventh-place finish. His time in W12 came to end in 2006 when he was punished and placed on gardening leave for expressing an interest in the Leicester City post. Spells at Plymouth Argyle and Leicester City followed before leading Blackpool to the Premier League for the first time in 2010.

Neil Warnock

One of football's most colourful managers and master motivator, Neil Warnock became Rangers FIFTH manager of a roller-coaster of a season in March 2010, after resigning from London rivals Crystal Palace. Coinciding with the arrival of new Chairman Ishan Saksena, Warnock kicked off his reign with a 3–1 win over promotion contenders West Bromwich Albion and steered Rangers away from the relegation zone, culminating in a 2–0 win at Selhurst Park over his former club. That summer Warnock reshaped the QPR squad, getting rid of the raft of loan players and bringing in reliable pros like Shaun Derry and Paddy Kenny, as well as securing maverick Adel Taarabt on a permanent basis. The transformation was immediate with Rangers going thirteen games unbeaten at the start of a campaign that saw the side top the table for all but two weeks of the season. Promotion was secured with a 2–0 win over Watford in April 2011, just over a year after he took charge, marking Rangers' return to the top flight for the first time in sixteen years. Often controversial but highly successful, Warnock led QPR into the Premier League citing that this would be his final job before bringing the curtain down on a career that has seen him manage twelve clubs and achieve seven promotions.

DID YOU KNOW?

While a player at Spurs, Alex Stock also trained as a banker in the event his football career came to an end.

Dave Sexton was the son of former professional boxer Archie Sexton, and boxed himself as a teenager.

Terry Venables is accomplished singer and even released a single in the build-up to the 2010 World Cup.

In 2006 Holloway came fifteenth in a *Time Out* magazine poll to determine London's funniest personality, ahead of Paul Merton and Ali G.

No stranger to confrontation, Neil Warnock's Wikipedia page includes a list of every player, manager, referee and fan whom he's ever fallen out with.

STAR WRITE-UP

The QPR section of *FourFourTwo* magazine's 1995/96 season preview was partly written by a 17-year-old future lead singer of The Libertines and Babyshambles, Pete Doherty.

MANIC MONDAY

QPR's match with Manchester City on 17 August 1992 was the first ever game to be shown live as part of Sky's new *Monday Night Football*. The game, which ended in a 1–1 draw thanks to Andy Sinton's second-half equaliser, was given the full big-match experience, with dancing cheerleaders and sky divers and a series of pyrotechnics. Sinton also featured in Sky's advertising campaign to launch their Premier League coverage, alongside the likes of Gordon Strachan, future QPR defender Vinnie Jones and Darren Anderton.

MASCOT MAYHEM

The pre-match entertainment at Loftus Road usually consists of a hot dog and a trip to the Rodney Marsh bar, but for the young Rangers fans (and some of the older ones) there's always the appearance of the perennial club mascot walking round the side of the pitch to put a smile on people's faces. And Rangers now find themselves onto their third different mascot.

Archie

Having a badge that doesn't feature an animal or a nickname that's not shared with a fictional creature, Rangers' first mascot was a simple but effective character – a giant football. First appearing in the mid-1990s, the larger than life soccer sphere was given the name 'Archie' as an apparent play on the 'R' in QPR and the club's nickname the Rs.

Jude

Rangers have Gerry Francis to thank for the creation of Jude the Cat as club mascot, from his second spell as QPR manager in 1998. Francis took over a team struggling at the wrong end of the First Division but managed to turn the team around with a string of results in November of that year that coincided with the arrival of a stray black cat at Loftus Road. Christened 'Jude' as a throwback to the club's original name, the magical moggy won Francis the Manager of the Month trophy and helped Rangers secure their First Division status that season. The following campaign the club honoured the new lucky charm with a 6ft black cat of their own as the club's new official mascot, a position the friendly feline held until 2009.

Spark

It wasn't just the badge and the ground Flavio Briatore revamped upon taking a seat among the QPR hierarchy in 2007 – he also got rid of the mascot too. With black cats seen as a sign of bad luck in Briatore's homeland of Italy, the eccentric new owner got rid of Jude and in his place came a more ferocious feline, Spark the tiger. Taking his name from the 's' on Queens and 'Park' in the club's name, the story fed to Rangers' young fans was that in the summer of 2009 Jude went travelling and while on safari met Spark and told him all about a wonderful football club called QPR. So excited was he, that he begged Jude to let him take over mascot duties and swapped the safari for Shepherd's Bush in time for the start of the 2008/09 season – where he remained a figure of fun on matchdays until September 2011.

Jude

New owner Tony Fernandes signalled his intent to remove any remnants of the previous regime by bringing back Jude as mascot ahead of the home game with Newcastle United on 12 September 2011.

LOFTUS ROAD LEGEND – RODNEY MARSH

Alec Stock paid just £15,000 for Fulham's top scorer in March 1966, in what looked like a bargain buy and Marsh made his debut in a 1–1 at Peterborough, where his sole contribution was a booking. A week later, however, on his home debut it took Rodney just 3 minutes to get on the score sheet in a 6–1 win over Millwall. He would go onto to score 8 goals in just 18 starts that season and quickly became a favourite with the Rangers crowd.

The following campaign, Marsh's first full season, was truly memorable as he would go onto score 30 of QPR's 108 league goals in a season that saw Rangers win promotion to the Second Division and become the first third-tier side to win the League Cup – Marsh scoring a memorable goal in the 3–2 win over West Brom at Wembley. His total of 44 goals in all competitions remains a club record that has yet to be beaten. A successive promotion followed with Marsh netting 14 goals in 15 games in an injury-hit campaign as Rangers moved into the top flight of English football for the first time. Alec Stock resigned prior to the 1968/69 season and it saw a disappointing campaign follow with Rangers finishing bottom of the league and Marsh netting just 4 times. However, over the next 2 years Rangers established themselves once again in Division Two with Marsh scoring a further 44 goals and earning his first England cap against Switzerland in November 1971. His goalscoring exploits eventually started to attract the so-called bigger sides and when Manchester City bid £200,000 for the maverick number 10 in March 1972, it was seen as too big an offer to refuse and Marsh left the club having scored 106 goals in 211 appearances.

A slow start at City saw fingers pointed that his arrival upset the dressing room and prevented the club from winning the league title, but Marsh soon turned things around and became a hero at Maine Road in the same way he had done in W12. After City, Marsh moved to the fledgling American league to play for Tampa Bay Rowdies before a famous spell at Fulham alongside George Best. He retired in 1979 and played indoor football for the Rowdies and later become a well-known TV pundit for *Sky Sports*. More recently Marsh has appeared in reality TV shows including 2007's *I'm a Celebrity Get Me Out of Here* (where he finished fifth), *Come Dine With Me* and

Celebrity Coach Trip where the former Rangers number 10 was partnered up with 1980s pop star Cheryl Baker.

DID YOU KNOW?

A picture of Marsh in a Manchester City shirt appears on the cover of Oasis' 1994 debut album *Definitely Maybe*.

QPR TIMELINE – 1950s & 1960s

1952 – Rangers relegated to Third Division South.

1953 – QPR changed their kit to plain white shorts and blue shorts.

1959 – Rangers became members of the newly formed Third Division of the Football League; Alec Stock became QPR manager.

1960 – Kit colours reverted back to the more familiar blue and white hoops.

1963 – Tony Ingham retired having played 555 times for the club.

1964 – Jim Gregory joined the QPR board and was elected chairman of the club.

1965 – Rodney Marsh signed for QPR in a £15,000 deal from Fulham; Frank Sibley became Rangers' first ever substitute.

1967 – The club won the League Cup with a 3–2 win over West Bromwich Albion at Wembley and won the Third Division championship.

1968 – Finished runners-up to Ipswich Town in Division Two and won promotion to the top flight; South Africa Road stand built at Loftus Road.

1969 – Rangers' first season in the First Division ended in disappointment when they were relegated with the league's lowest ever points total (18).

FIVE GREAT GOALS

Rodney Marsh v West Bromwich Albion
4 March 1967, League Cup final
A goal on QPR's most famous day from one of the great Rangers players – the maverick Rodney Marsh and his strike in the 1967 League Cup final. Receiving the ball 30 yards from goal, Marsh skipped past two defenders before sliding the ball in off the post and past West Brom custodian Dick Sheppard – a goal truly worthy of a memorable occasion in the club's history.

Gerry Francis v Liverpool
16 August 1975, First Division
A move that was symbolic of a side that ran Liverpool so close to the title that season. Ironically this goal was scored against the Reds on the opening day of the campaign and would later be voted as the BBC's Goal of the Season. A move that started from Phil Parkes in the QPR goal and included a cheeky backheel from Stan Bowles, found Francis in the middle of the park. One well-timed one-two with Don Givens later, Francis slotted the ball home from the right-hand side of the penalty box. The strike helped Rangers to their first ever win over the Merseyside outfit and set the tone for a memorable season.

Clive Allen v West Ham United
31 March 1984, First Division

The Allen family have left a legacy of memories spanning four decades at Loftus Road (see page 54), but no goal was better than this one from Clive. Receiving the ball on the edge of the penalty area, Allen found himself under pressure from two defenders in claret and blue. The striker didn't panic and bamboozled both players with a series of wonderfully skilled drag-backs and a flick that gave him just enough time and space to slide the ball past the Hammers' keeper. It would be one of 15 goals that the Rangers front man contributed in the club's return to the top flight.

Roy Wegerle v Leeds United
20 October 1990, First Division

A special goal from a special player who epitomsed what it meant to wear the number 10 shirt for QPR. Picking the ball up on the right flank, Wegerle nipped past the first defender, put it through the legs of the next, fooled another with some clever footwork and outfought two more United players, before his mazy run ended with a shot into the bottom corner. The goal won the American international the ITV Goal of the Season and was a wonderful example of the talent Wegerle possessed.

Trevor Sinclair v Barnsley
25 February 1997, FA Cup fourth round

For a player who played in the Premier League for the majority of his career and represented England at the 2002 World Cup, it's a surprise that Sinclair will be best remembered for a goal in an unattractive FA Cup tie against Barnsley – but this was no ordinary goal. John Spencer crossed a long hopeful ball towards Sinclair who – with his back to goal – instinctively caught the ball with a bicycle-kick volley that dipped over the Barnsley keeper and into the back of the net from fully 20 yards. The goal was so good it later beat David Beckham's famous halfway line effort to win BBC's Goal of the Season accolade.

TV STARS

Due to its close proximity to the BBC studios in West London, QPR have enjoyed an amusing relationship with the TV channel and have been referred to in a number of the BBC's most popular comedy shows. Most famous was the 1990s sitcom *Bottom*, where Ade Edmondson played lead character and QPR fan Eddie Hitler, and the club are mentioned throughout the show's three series and live shows. It has led to the perception that Edmondson is a real-life QPR fan, when he is actually an Exeter City follower who has a box at London rivals Chelsea. Other notable QPR references to have appeared in BBC shows include *Men Behaving Badly* (with a poster of the 1996/96 team donning the walls of the characters' flat), *Steptoe and Son*, *Red Dwarf* and more recently *My Family* where lead character Ben (played by Robert Lindsay) is seen in one episode dressed in blue and white and shouting 'C'mon you Hoops' at the television. *Little Britain* creation 'Emily' has also proclaimed on a number of occasions to have played left-back for QPR.

In 1991, the BBC went one step further with their QPR connection with comedy-drama *Boys From The Bush*. Starring Tim Healy, the series followed his character Reg Toomer as an ex-pat from Shepherd's Bush now living in Australia. Although set in Melbourne the show constantly referenced QPR and the series ended with a scene from inside Loftus Road.

Away from the BBC, satellite kids' channel Nickelodeon also filmed an episode of popular late 1990s show *Renford Rejects* at Loftus Road, in a scene where lead character Jason Summerbee got to play in front of a full Loftus Road crowd and take on Rangers legend Stan Bowles.

INTERNATIONAL STAGE

Loftus Road has played host to a number of internationals over the years as well as being the European home ground for Australia. The ground has yet to hold a full England international, although it did host a memorable 'B' international in 1998 that included a goal set up by former winger Trevor Sinclair and scored by former front man Les Ferdinand.

Here's a list of all internationals staged at Loftus Road:

18 February 1992	England B 3–0 France B
21 April 1998	England B 4–1 Russia B
26 March 2002	Nigeria 1–1 Paraguay
18 May 2002	Nigeria 1–0 Jamaica
21 May 2004	Australia 1–0 South Africa
28 February 2006	Trinidad & Tobago 2–0 Iceland
14 November 2006	Australia 1–1 Ghana
6 February 2007	Australia 1–3 Denmark
19 August 2008	Australia 2–2 South Africa
31 March 2009	England U20 2–0 Italy U20
3 March 2010	South Korea 2–0 Ivory Coast

HAIR-RAISING

Arthur Longbottom may have been one of QPR's star forwards of the 1950s but the Yorkshireman was also a dab hand with a pair of scissors too – and even trained to be a hairdresser. Spending afternoons in a local barbers, Longbottom would often give his fellow Rangers team-mates haircuts and wet shaves and was called 'a natural' by the shop's owner.

ALL KITTED OUT

1974 marked the first time a visible logo was seen on a QPR shirt apart from the club badge, with the logo of kit manufacturer Admiral. Eight years later, Rangers would agree their first kit sponsorship deal with brewery firm Guinness. This is a complete list of the companies they have produced and sponsored QPR's kits.

Season	Kit Manufacturer	Sponsor
1974/75	Admiral	
1975/76	Umbro	
1976/77	Adidas	
1977/78	Adidas	
1978/79	Adidas	
1979/80	Adidas	
1980/81	Adidas	
1981/82	Adidas	
1983/84	Adidas	Guinness
1984/85	Adidas	Guinness
1985/86	Adidas	Guinness
1986/87	Adidas	Blue Star
1987/88	Adidas	Holland Fly KLM
1988/89	Adidas	Holland Fly KLM
1989/90	Influence	Holland Fly KLM
1990/91	Influence	Influence Leisurewear
1991/92	Brooks	Brooks
1992/93	Rangers Clubhouse	Classic FM

Season	Kit Manufacturer	Sponsor
1993/94	Rangers Clubhouse	CSF (Computer Software and Finance)
1994/95	Rangers Clubhouse	Compaq
1995/96	View From	Compaq
1996/97	View From	Ericsson
1997/98	Le Coq Sportif	Ericsson
1999/00	Le Coq Sportif	Ericsson
2000/01	Le Coq Sportif	Ericsson
2001/02	Le Coq Sportif	JD Sports
2002/03	Le Coq Sportif	JD Sports
2003/04	Le Coq Sportif	Binatone
2004/05	Le Coq Sportif	Binatone
2005/06	Le Coq Sportif	Binatone
2006/07	Le Coq Sportif	Cargiant.co.uk
2007/08	Le Coq Sportif	Cargiant.co.uk
2008/09	Lotto	Gulf Air
2009/10	Lotto	Gulf Air
2010/11	Lotto	Gulf Air
2011/12	Lotto	Malaysia Airlines/Air Asia

LOFTUS ROAD LEGEND – GERRY FRANCIS

A product of Rangers' successful youth team, Francis made his debut for QPR as a 17-year-old during a 2–1 defeat to Liverpool in 1968 and a year later made his first start in a 3–1 win over Portsmouth – marking the occasion with his first senior goal for the club. Manager Les Allen had tried to ease the youngster into the first team but by the time Gordon Jago took over in 1971, Francis was too good to leave out and was given the number 8 shirt permanently. From then on he became a regular fixture in the first team and the main creative spark in midfield, striking up almost telepathic understandings with Stan Bowles and Don Givens. By the 1975/76 season, Francis was a pivotal part of Dave Sexton's free-flowing attractive Rangers side that pushed the mighty Liverpool all the way in the title race, but agonisingly missed out on the championship by one point. Francis earned international recognition too, earning 12 caps and captaining his country on 8 occasions.

A back injury the following season then robbed Rangers of their midfield maestro and he would only play 24 of Rangers' next 84 games, as he struggled to discover the kind of form that had made him a Loftus Road hero. In 1979, Francis ended a decade in W12 by moving across London to Crystal Palace. However, he never settled at Selhurst Park, and despite making over 50 appearances for the Eagles he soon moved back to QPR. The back injury, though, was still taking its toll and Francis soon moved on again to enjoy spells at Coventry City, Exeter City, Swansea City and Bristol Rovers before moving into management.

Cutting his managerial teeth at Exeter he spent just a season at St James' Park before taking over at Bristol Rovers, turning a struggling Third Division side into a respected passing team a division above. It wasn't long before the lure of Loftus Road was too much to ignore and he returned to QPR as manager in 1992, succeeding Don Howe. Having inherited a squad with talent such as Alan McDonald, Andy Sinton and Les Ferdinand, Francis got the best out of Rangers and bought the likes of Gary Penrice, Ian Holloway and Darren Peacock with him to make his own mark on the team. All of this paid dividends when he led the Rs to a fifth-place finish in the newly created Premier League – their best position since 1984 and as London's top club. Successive mid-table finishes followed and Francis unearthed gems like Trevor Sinclair and Bradley Allen and made Ferdinand a Premier League star. Unfortunately, a clash with the board over a possible appointment of Rodney Marsh above him led to him leaving Loftus Road in 1994 and he took over at Tottenham Hotspur. At White Hart Lane he helped the club to seventh spot and an FA Cup semi-final but mid-table finishes the following two campaigns saw the Spurs board unconvinced and he resigned in November 1997.

A year later he was back at QPR, who had slumped since his departure and were now in a relegation battle at the bottom of

Division One. The Francis effect was enough for Rangers to pull off the great escape that season, sealing it with a 6–0 win over Palace on the last day. But with no money to spend and an ever-decreasing quality of squad, he resigned from his post in February 2001 with relegation to the third tier imminent.

A further spell at Bristol Rovers followed before Gerry took a 7-year break from the game. He is now currently on the coaching staff at Stoke City and occasionally appears as a pundit on Sky Sports.

DID YOU KNOW?

Gerry took part in *Fantasy Football*'s famous 'Phoenix From The Flames' sketch in 1997, recreating his two England goals in a 1975 fixture against Scotland.

BOWLED OVER

Stan Bowles was often regarded as something of a character both on and off the pitch and one notable incident in his playing days involved the famous FA Cup trophy. Having won the FA Cup competition 4 days earlier, Sunderland were parading the trophy at Roker Park on 9 May 1973, when they met QPR on the last day of the Division Two season. The trophy had been placed on a table at the side of the pitch when Bowles kicked the ball at it full speed, sending the cup flying through the air. The crowd predictably went ballistic, but Stan had the last laugh by scoring a brace in the match which ended in a pitch invasion. Bowles has said of the incident:

> I can remember it like it was yesterday. It was May 1973, QPR's game at Sunderland had been delayed because of the Cup final that year, which Sunderland had won with a fluky win against Leeds. We had to play them on the Monday

afterwards. They paraded the cup around then left it on the table on the halfway line. A guy called Tony Hazell and I had a little bet who could hit it with the ball, it was just a spontaneous thing. I did it during the warm-up and it didn't go down very well. I ran straight across the park and then, bang! The FA Cup went shooting up in the air. I believe the cup got dented but not sure if it was Hazell that done it or I did; it didn't matter though, once it was done, it was done.

During the game I was winding up all their players who had probably all had a drink over the weekend and we beat them 3–0. I scored two goals and almost caused a riot by taking the piss. I was going up to their players and asking them 'how the f**k did you beat Leeds?' It was on the headlines on *News at 10* – we had to be taken off the pitch for half an hour as all their fans ran on the pitch and delayed the end of the game.

I was playing really well at the time and it was a nuisance having to go up to Sunderland on a Monday night for the last game of the season. It was an easy win and when on form I could be a bit arrogant. As far as I can recall, it was just after half time when all the Sunderland people jumped over the fence and ran onto the pitch and we had to be taken off. They came from behind the goal like a swarm. Some of them were coming at me but luckily enough I was right near the touchline and managed to get off quick and into the dressing room. It was like a load of wildebeest coming at you.

Our chairman Jim Gregory wanted to call the game off but we had to go back on after about 40 minutes. We didn't go out on the town afterwards that's for sure. Not that I had any interest in going out in Sunderland, we just stayed in the hotel and drank. It all just got a bit out of hand, I didn't know they were all mad up there. I've never spoken to any of the Sunderland players and I won't be doing work up there. I know a lot of people in Newcastle and they tell me, 'Don't go to Sunderland Stan, they've got long memories and they don't like you.'

THE ALLEN FAMILY

No family have a closer connection to Queens Park Rangers than the Allens; Les, Clive, Martin and Bradley. Covering four decades, the four men enjoyed significant careers at Loftus Road beginning with Les in 1965 and ending with Bradley's departure 1996.

Les Allen (1965–71)

In something of a shock move, Les Allen joined Third Division QPR from top-flight side Spurs in July 1965, convinced by chairman Jim Gregory that he was joining a club very much on the up. A cultured centre forward, Allen's experienced head among a young Rangers team saw a progression in the team's style of play, one that would become synonymous with Rs teams of the future. In his second season at the club, Allen was part of the side that famously beat West Brom in the 1967 League Cup final and achieved promotion to the Second Division. Allen retired at the end of the 1968/69 season and briefly took over as manager at QPR before moving to become a scout at Swindon Town.

Clive Allen (1978–80 and 1981–4)

It didn't take long for Les' son Clive to make an impact in an Rs shirt, announcing his arrival with a hat-trick on his full debut in a 5–1 win over Coventry in November 1978. Though he couldn't prevent Rangers from being relegated that season he went on to score 28 goals the following campaign earning himself a £1.25 million transfer to Arsenal. He would spend just two months at Highbury however, bizarrely moving to Crystal Palace before returning to Loftus Road in 1981 under the guidance of Terry Venables. His goals in his second spell in W12 helped the club reach the 1982 FA Cup final and promotion back to the First Division a season later. Allen earned his first England cap while still a QPR player before moving on to Spurs in 1984 with a record of 83 goals in 158 games for Rangers.

Martin Allen (1984–9)

Clive's cousin Martin was the next Allen to don the blue and white hoops, progressing through the youth ranks to make his debut in October 1984. Unlike his relations before him, Martin was a tough-tackling all-action midfielder who would go on to earn the nickname 'Mad Dog' due to his competitive nature. During his 5 years at Loftus Road Martin earned England U21 honours and was part of the Rangers team that lost to Oxford United in the 1986 League Cup final. A £650,000 transfer to West Ham brought his career in West London to an end, having made 167 appearances and scoring 19 goals for the Super Hoops.

Bradley Allen (1989–96)

Younger brother to Clive, Bradley became the fourth Allen family member to play for QPR when he made his Rangers debut in January 1989. A more technical and skilful type of striker than his older brother, although not as prolific, Bradley played 94 times for Rangers scoring 34 goals during an era that saw Rangers finish as the country's top London club in the newly formed Premier League. His hat-trick at Goodison Park in November 1993 remains one of Rangers' best individual performances away from Loftus Road. Bradley left after 7 seasons to join London rivals Charlton Athletic and later played for Grimsby Town and Bristol Rovers.

DID YOU KNOW?

Now long-retired from the game, Les Allen is a model maker who splits his time between Hornchurch and Souni-Zanakia in Cyprus.

In 1997 Clive Allen turned his hand to another sport, appearing for American football team London Monarchs as a kicker.

As a manager, some of Martin Allen's unusual training methods included making his Brentford team swim up a cold river and conducting a Notts County training session by the side of the road en route to Yeovil.

Bradley shares his birthday (17 September) with fashion icon Stella McCartney and former Wimbledon champion Goran Ivanisevic.

HELPING HANDS

QPR fans have always been willing supporters and on hand to help out the club whenever they can. In 1934, upon the formation of the first Queens Park Rangers Supporters' Club, the members raised £100 for the club to help pay for crush barriers on the terracing and to pay for the trainer's equipment. Two years later another £1,500 was handed over to pay for the new roof on the Loftus Road end of the ground. In more modern times, supporters Alex and Matthew Winton agreed to help the club sign both Ebeli 'Doudou' Mbombo in 2001 and Danny Shittu a year later. The pair, who were the owners of Ghosts Menswear, agreed to sponsor the first year of the players' wages and cover any accommodation costs.

QPR TIMELINE – 1970s & 1980s

1970 – Phil Parkes signed from Walsall for £15,000.

1971 – Rodney Marsh became the first QPR player for 64 years to be capped by England.

1972 – Stan Bowles signed for QPR from Carlisle United.

1973 – QPR finished runners-up in Division Two and were promoted.

1974 – Loftus Road set a new attendance record of 35,353 in a match against Leeds United; Dave Sexton replaced Gordon Jago as manager; Stan Bowles scored for England in a 2–0 win over Wales – the first England goal scored by a QPR player.

1976 – QPR finished a point behind Liverpool as Division One runners-up, their highest ever league position; Gerry Francis won goal of the season for his strike against Liverpool.

1977 – Rangers competed in Europe for the first time in their history, reaching the UEFA Cup quarter-finals.

1979 – Phil Parkes moved to West Ham for £565,000 – a world record fee for a goalkeeper. QPR finished twentieth and were relegated to Division Two.

1980 – Terry Venables appointed QPR manager.

1981 – QPR installed a plastic pitch at Loftus Road, the first in English football, at a cost of £350,000.

1982 – The club made their first and only FA Cup final, but after a 1–1 draw lost the replay to Tottenham.

1983 – Rangers won the Division Two championship, with a 10-point margin over Wolverhampton Wanderers.

1983 – Brewery firm Guinness were the first name to appear on Rangers shirts as kit sponsors.

1984 – Finished fifth in Division One and qualified for the UEFA Cup; Terry Venables left to manage Barcelona.

1986 – QPR under Jim Smith reached the Milk Cup (League Cup) final but were beaten 3–0 by Oxford United. Alan McDonald became the first QPR player to play in a World Cup for Northern Ireland.

1988 – 24-year-old Richard Thompson became chairman of the club.

1989 – Roy Wegerle became QPR's first £1 million buy, joining from Luton Town.

EUROPEAN TOUR

In 1912 QPR played their first games outside of England when they travelled to France and Germany to play a series of exhibition matches. They first met Fulham in Paris for the Dubonnet Trophy, but having only arrived in the country at 7 a.m. that day, the team unsurprisingly lost 4–1. After playing one more game in France, Rangers moved on to Germany where they played six games, winning all six by an aggregate score of 40–7. The results were Paris Red Star 9–2, Saarbrücken 12–1, Kaiserslautern 1–0, Mannheim 3–0, Pforzheim 7–3, Nuremberg 5–1 and Stuttgart 12–1.

MODEL CLUB

While dating notorious QPR fan and Babyshambles singer Pete Doherty, supermodel Kate Moss appeared in the sleeve notes for *Down in Albion* dressed in just a QPR shirt. Other instances of model-related QPR links include Claudia Schiffer bizarrely appearing with a Rangers scarf and Germany flag on the official website, and Naomi Campbell and Tamara Beckwith attending a game on behalf of then owner Flavio Briatore in October 2007.

FAMOUS FIVE

When Don Revie named his England squad for the European Championship game with Portugal in November 1975, there were five QPR players in his 22-man party – the most ever call-ups in one go for the club. Stan Bowles, Dave Thomas, Gerry Francis, Phil Parkes and Ian Gillard were the chosen five.

LIGHTS ON

The first ever QPR game to be held under floodlights came on 5 October 1953 as Rangers hosted Arsenal at Loftus Road. A crowd of 16,028 saw the game in which film and TV star Pat Kirkwood kicked off the match and Arsenal won 3–1.

1967 AND ALL THAT ...

The 1967 League Cup win remains the only major trophy won by QPR in the club's history. This is a round-by-round summary of that famous cup run that culminated in Rangers' most famous hour.

Round One v Colchester United

Having drawn their first league game of the season 3 days earlier against Shrewsbury Town, Rangers were paired with fellow Third Division side Colchester United in the first round of the sixth League Cup competition. FIFA President Sir Stanley Rous was in attendance to turn on the new Loftus Road floodlights in front of a crowd of 5,497. The game proved to be a one-sided affair as Rodney Marsh netted 4 goals and Mark Lazarus a fifth in a 5–0 romp over the Essex club.

Round Two v Aldershot Town

By September Rangers were eighth in the league and headed to the Recreation Ground to face Fourth Division Aldershot off the back of a 2–2 draw with Reading at Elm Park. In a closely fought match, Aldershot took the lead before Les Allen equalised before the break. A goalless second half meant a replay back at Loftus Road a week later, with Rangers winning thanks to a penalty from Jim Langley and a Rodney Marsh goal.

Round Three v Swansea Town

Rangers reached the third round for the first time in their history and were drawn with Swansea Town. The two sides had just met in the league, with QPR defeating the Welsh side 4–2 and moving into second place in Division Three, just behind leaders Bournemouth. A crowd of 13,000 attended the game that saw Swansea take the lead in the 32nd minute when Ivor Allchurch rounded two defenders and fired past Peter Springett in the Rangers goal. On the hour mark QPR equalised with a Tony Hazell shot that deflected off Brian Purcell, and with a minute to go Mike Keen headed the winner to send QPR into the fourth round.

Round Four v Leicester City

The reward for reaching round four was a match against First Division Leicester City at Loftus Road, a draw that attracted a crowd of nearly 21,000 to see the Third Division league leaders try to upset the odds. Roger Morgan opened the scoring for the Rs in the 21st minute, but the visitors were level within a minute thanks to Derek Dougan, and Dougan netted again to give Leicester a 2–1 lead at the break. Rangers came out fighting in the second half and were back in it after 56 minutes when Les Allen's chipped shot hit the crossbar and went in off World Cup-winning goalkeeper Gordon Banks. A minute later, Rangers regained the lead when Keith Sanderson released Mark Lazarus and his cross was met by Allen who finished clinically. Lazarus then killed the game with a fourth to see Rangers take their place among the last eight.

Quarter-final v Carlisle United

Second Division league leaders Carlisle were Rangers' quarter-final opponents and another big crowd of almost 20,000 flocked to Loftus Road to see if the Rs could continue their impressive cup run. Once again Rangers proved themselves capable of matching higher company as Rodney Marsh's brace was enough to see off United and put QPR through to the semi-finals.

Semi-final v Birmingham City

The draw for the two-legged semi-finals saw QPR paired with Birmingham City, and West Bromwich Albion meeting West Ham United, giving the possibility of an all-Birmingham or all-London League Cup final. Rangers travelled to St Andrews for the first leg still top of the Third Division and beaten only twice in the previous 34 matches in all competitions. Barry Bridge gave Birmingham a half-time lead, but no Rangers fan was prepared for what was to come in the second half, as goals from Rodney Marsh, Roger Morgan, Mark Lazarus and Les Allen saw Rangers record a 4–1 win – one the finest away performances in the club's history. With a 3-goal lead in the bag Rangers dominated the second leg and goals from Rodney Marsh (2) and Mike Keen gave them a 7–2 aggregate win over Birmingham and meant they would play West Bromwich Albion as the first Third Division side to ever reach a League Cup final.

Final v West Bromwich Albion

A record 97,952 crowd attended Wembley Stadium on 4 March 1967 for the League Cup final between Third Division Queens Park Rangers and First Division West Bromwich Albion. It was the Baggies who raced into a 2–0 lead through Clive Clark, but a second-half fight-back from Rangers saw Roger Morgan, Rodney Marsh and Mark Lazarus etch their names into Rangers folklore with the goals that gave QPR their only major trophy to date.

MOVES TO MERGE – I

In the summer of 1968 the idea to merge Rangers with another club was talked about for the first time. Due to his desire to have a First Division stadium, the then QPR chairman Jim Gregory held discussions with local rivals Brentford with a view to merging the two clubs. The new club would use Brentford's more modern Griffin Park ground as it had a capacity of 40,000. Fans of both clubs opposed the move and after just a few preliminary meetings, the idea was dropped. Gregory instead put all his efforts into turning Rangers' Loftus Road ground into a top-flight standard stadium.

THE 92 MAN

While manager of Queens Park Rangers, Jim Smith became the first boss to manage at all 92 league grounds during a match against Leicester City in April 1986. To help him celebrate the milestone, Rangers ran out 4–1 winners with goals from Clive Allen, Gary Bannister, John Byrne and Michael Robinson. It was in a season when QPR finished thirteenth in the league and reached the League Cup final, losing to Oxford United.

ADVERT ADVANTAGE

In February 1972, a football commercial was screened on TV for the very first time, when ITV ran an advert for the friendly between QPR and West Bromwich Albion. The game had been arranged at very little notice and having only publicised it once, over the PA system in the previous week's game at Luton Town, only twelve tickets had been sold for the match. With the club hoping for a gate of 7,000–8,000, Chairman Jim Gregory suggested the club explore the possibility of a TV commercial. The advert starring Rangers' Rodney Marsh, was shown on Thursday 3 February at 6.55 in the evening and results exceeded all expectations, with a non-stop queue forming the next day at the box office. Ironically the ad received further publicity in the newspapers helping the game reach its attendance target as 7,087 fans witnessed the match in which West Brom beat the Rs 2–1. Despite reports of the ad costing £750, the true cost was just £192.50 spilt between the two sides.

QPR TIMELINE – 1990s & 2000s

1990 – Paul Parker played for England in the 1990 World Cup finals in Italy; Roy Wegerle won goal of the season for his solo effort against Leeds United.

1991 – Gerry Francis returned to the club as manager.

1992 – QPR recorded a 4–1 win over Manchester United at Old Trafford; The club were one of 22 founding members of the FA Premier League; Les Ferdinand made his England debut.

1993 – A fifth-place finish in the Premier League meant QPR were London's top club.

1995 – Gerry Francis resigned due to a boardroom dispute; Les Ferdinand joined Newcastle for a club record sale of £6 million.

1996 – Rangers ended a 13-year stay in the top flight when they finished in nineteenth place and were relegated under Ray Wilkins.

1997 – Richard Thompson sold the club to Chrysalis boss Chris Wright; Wasps rugby club begin sharing Loftus Road with Rangers; Trevor Sinclair's spectacular overhead-kick was voted goal of the season.

1998 – Mike Sheron joined the club for a record £2.35 million fee from Stoke City.

1999 – Gerry Francis joined for a second spell as manager and prevented relegation to Division Two on goals scored.

2000 – Francis resigned and was replaced by Ian Holloway but he couldn't prevent the club from being relegated to the third tier of English football.

2001 – QPR entered administration amid financial difficulties at the club.

2003 – Rangers reached the Division Two play-off final but lost 1–0 to Cardiff City after extra time.

2004 – QPR were promoted to the newly branded Championship after finishing runners-up to Plymouth Argyle.

2006 – Ian Holloway was placed on gardening leave and eventually replaced by coach Gary Waddock.

2007 – Motor racing millionaires Flavio Briatore and Bernie Ecclestone took over the club, along with a 20 per cent share taken by Lakshmi Mittal.

2009 – Briatore oversaw the hiring and firing of managers John Gregory, Luigi De Canio, Iain Dowie, Paulo Sousa, Jim Magilton and Paul Hart in just eighteen months.

2010 – Neil Warnock appointed as manager and saved club from relegation.

2011 – Rangers led the Championship for all but two weeks of the season and were promoted to the Premier League, 16 years after their last appearance; Tony Fernandes bought the club from Flavio Briatore and Bernie Ecclestone; Tommy Smith scored Rangers' first goal back in the top flight in a 1–0 win at Everton.

NEXT GOAL WINS

One of the earliest instances of the 'golden goal' rule came in a Division Three South Cup match between QPR and Bournemouth in May 1946. The Rs had taken the tie to a replay after a 1–1 draw at Dean Court, but after 90 minutes and three periods of extra time it was decided that whoever got the next goal would win. In the end it was the Cherries' Jack Kirkham who netted the winner 4 minutes into the fourth period of extra time, winning the tie for Bournemouth. The game lasted a total of 136 minutes.

INTERNATIONALS

The following is a list of every full and Under 21 international cap earned by players while playing for QPR.

Canada – Marc Bircham (4)

Czech Republic – Jan Stejskal (3)

Denmark U21 – Kurt Bakholt (1)

England – Clive Allen (3), David Bardsley (2), Stan Bowles (5), Dave Clement (5), Terry Fenwick (19), Les Ferdinand (7), Gerry Francis (12), Ian Gillard (3), John Gregory (6), Evelyn Lintott (3), Rodney Marsh (1), Paul Parker (16), Phil Parkes (1), David Seaman (3), Andy Sinton (10), Dave Thomas (8)

England U21 – Bradley Allen (8), Clive Allen (3), Martin Allen (2), Dexter Blackstock (2), Clarke Carlisle (3), Trevor Challis (2), Dean Coney (1), Daniele Dichio (1), Terry Fenwick (11), Wayne Fereday (5), Kevin Gallen (4), Peter Hucker (2), Andy Impey (1), David Kerslake (1), Paul Murray (4), Phil Parkes (1), Chris Plummer (5), Nigel Quashie (4), Trevor Sinclair (13), Steve Wicks (1), Chris Woods (3)

Hungary – Akos Buzsaky (9)

Iceland – Heidar Helguson (5),

Ireland – Ray Brady (6), John Byrne (13), Damien Delaney (2), Don Givens (27), Walter Greer (3), Paul McGee (9), Terry Mancini (4), Neil Murphy (3), Mick O'Brien (2), Michael Robinson (6), Martin Rowlands (5), Gary Waddock (18), Mick Walsh (4)

Ireland U21 – Steve Gallen (3)

Jamaica – Richard Langley (8), Damion Stewart (14)

Latvia – Kaspars Gorkss (14)

Morocco – Adel Taarabt (12)

Nigeria – Danny Shittu (1)

Northern Ireland – Colin Clarke (5), Iain Dowie (13), Billy Hamilton (1), David McCreey (9), Alan McDonald (52), Steve Morrow (14), Keith Rowland (6), Ian Stewart (22)

Northern Ireland U21 – Richard Graham (15), Chris Heron (2), Terry McFlynn (7)

Pakistan – Zesh Rehman (1)

Scotland – Don Masson (14), John Spencer (1)

Scotland U21 – Paul Wright (1)

USA – Juergen Sommer (3)

Wales – Jeremy Charles (2), Leighton James (1), Robbie James (14), Paul Jones (5), Daniel Nardiello (2), Ivor Powell (5), Karl Ready (5), Tony Roberts (3), Danny Gabbidon (1)

Wales U21 – Leon Jeanne (8), Brian Law (2), Alan McCarthy (3), Michael Meaker (2), Karl Ready (6), Tony Roberts (2)

LOFTUS ROAD LEGEND – STAN BOWLES

Stanley Bowles started his career at Manchester City but his maverick behaviour didn't impress then boss Malcolm Allison and he was soon shipped out to first Bury, then Fourth Division Crewe Alexandra. His goals and skill in just one season at Gresty Road caught the attention of the bigger clubs and he was soon snapped up by Carlisle United. Now two leagues higher, United thought it would take time for Bowles to adapt to the league but he excelled and is still regarded as one of the best players ever to play for Carlisle.

Despite his displays, the team as a whole wasn't impressive and Ian MacFarlane, the man who bought Bowles to the club, was replaced by Alan Ashman. Bowles saw this as his opportunity to move on again, and to a team in the top flight where his talent belonged. So in September 1972, after scoring 13 goals in 36 games for the Cumbrians, Stan moved to Queens Park Rangers for £112,000, after manager Gordon Jago convinced Stan that his style of play would fit in perfectly with the likes of Gerry Francis and Terry Venables. Rangers fans had just seen their star player Rodney Marsh move on and were desperate for someone to replace him in the number 10 shirt – in Stan they found the perfect fit.

Over the next 7 years Bowles was part of the greatest ever Queens Park Rangers side and became the darling of Loftus Road, helping the Rs to second place in 1976, their highest ever league position. The following season Stan led Rangers into the UEFA Cup and showcased his unbelievable talent to the whole of Europe. He netted two hat-tricks in the first round against Brann Bergen before helping the Rs get all the way to the quarter-finals and finish as the tournament's top scorer with 11 goals. Of course much was made of Stan's off-pitch controversies, but on the pitch he had unbelievable skill and became one of the era's most entertaining players. While at Loftus Road, Bowles gained international recognition and played in Alf Ramsey's last game as England manager. Sadly, despite his mercurial talent he only gained 5 caps for his country, in an era that England really could have done with someone like him in the team.

Stan left the Super Hoops in 1979 to join Nottingham Forest and enjoyed further spells at Leyton Orient and Brentford before retiring in 1984. He can now be found as a regular down at Loftus Road and as an after-dinner speaker.

DID YOU KNOW?

Cornish band The Surgeons recorded a song on their 2010 album *Under the Knife* called 'I Saw Stan Bowles at B&Q'.

NOT UP FOR THE CUP

QPR are currently in the midst of the FA Cup's longest ever losing streak, having now gone a whole decade without winning a game in football's most prestigious cup competition. You have to go back to Rangers' Third Round win over Luton Town in 2001 to find their last victory, a year in which Bill Clinton was still President of the USA, England beat Germany 5–1 and Justin Bieber was only six years old.

The losing run:

2002	Round 1	Swansea City 4–0 QPR
2003	Round 1	Vauxhall Motors 0–0 QPR
	replay	QPR 1–1 Vauxhall Motors (Vauxhall Motors won 4–3 on penalties)
2004	Round 1	Grimsby Town 1–0 QPR
2005	Round 3	QPR 0–3 Nottingham Forest

2006	Round 3	Blackburn Rovers 3–0 QPR
2007	Round 3	QPR 2–2 Luton Town
	replay	Luton Town 1–0 QPR
2008	Round 3	Chelsea 1–0 QPR
2009	Round 3	QPR 0–0 Burnley
	replay	Burney 2–1 QPR (aet)
2010		Sheffield United 1–1 QPR
	replay	QPR 2–3 Sheffield United
2011	Round 3	Blackburn Rovers 1–0 QPR

CELEBRITY Rs

A plethora of famous faces from the entertainment industry are said to be QPR fans, including:

Howard Antony – Actor (*EastEnders*' Alan Jackson)
Bill Bailey – TV personality and comedian
Martin Clunes – Actor (*Men Behaving Badly* and *Doc Martin*)
Pete Doherty – Musician (The Libertines and Babyshambles)
Ashley Giles – Cricketer
Wendy James – Musician (Transvision Vamp)
Mick Jones – Musician (The Clash)
Michael Nyman – Composer
Jamie Oliver – TV Chef
Andrew Ridgley – Musician (Wham!)
Nick Cave – Musician
Glen Matlock – Musician (Sex Pistols)
Phil Collins – Musician (Genesis)
Alex Tudor – Cricketer
Dennis Wise – Former footballer
Delon Armitage – Rugby player
Anthony Wall – Golfer
Robert Smith – Musician (The Cure)

GREAT BRAWL OF CHINA

In February 2007 as part of their preparations for the 2008 Olympic Games, the Chinese football team went on a two-week tour of England that included a friendly against Rangers at their Harlington training ground. However, the match had to be abandoned after it descended into a 30-man brawl in which Chinese player Zheng Tao was knocked out and suffered a broken jaw in two places. In the aftermath of the event, assistant manager Richard Hill was suspended by the club.

MILITARY MAN

When Queens Park Rangers beat Mansfield Town 3–0 in March 1946, one of their goalscorers was a former army footballer and Military Medal winner, Danny Boxshall. As the former Acting Sergeant of the 53rd Reconnaissance Regiment, Royal Armoured Corps, Boxshall won the Military Medal while in charge of a Bren gun crew in north-west Germany. Boxshall was rewarded when commanding the lead reconnaissance car after his troop had been ordered to seize a bridge over the River Berkel in the town of Vreden. As he approached the bridge, his car was engaged by the enemy, but Boxshall simply ordered his driver to accelerate towards the Germans. The vehicle sped towards the bridge, Boxshall firing his Bren gun, while the remaining defenders threw down their arms and surrendered without destroying the valuable crossing point. After his heroics in the war, Boxshall would go onto score 18 goals in 40 games for QPR and win a Third Division South winners' medal before moving to Bristol City in 1948.

TEAM GB

At the end of the 1987/88 season QPR participated in an annual summer tournament in Korea, representing Great Britain against fifteen other teams made up of Olympic, national and club sides. The teams were spilt into four groups and Rangers faced the Olympic sides of USA, USSR and Nigeria. They drew with the US and Nigeria before losing 3–0 to the Soviet Union in front of crowds of up to 50,000.

FIVE MORE GREAT GAMES

QPR 1–1 Tottenham Hotspur
22 May 1982, FA Cup final
QPR's first and only FA Cup final appearance came under the guidance of Terry Venables, as Second Division QPR clashed with London rivals and holders Tottenham in the 1982 final. Just like in 1967, Rangers went in as underdogs but having seen off Middlesbrough, Blackpool, Grimsby Town, Crystal Palace and West Bromwich Albion, Venables' side were not to be taken lightly. A tense and tight match followed that featured very little in the way of goalmouth action and remained goalless at the end of normal time. On 109 minutes Glen Hoddle's deflected strike looked to have won it for the North Londoners, but with 5 minutes left Bob Hazell's nod on from a throw-in was headed home by Terry Fenwick, forcing Spurs to a replay and capping off an incredible effort from Venables' Rangers side.

QPR team: Hucker, Fenwick, Gillard, Waddock, Hazell, Roeder, Currie, Flanagan, Allen, Stainrod, Gregory

Liverpool 1–3 QPR
20 March 1991, First Division
Don Howe's side recorded the club's first ever win at Anfield with a fully deserved victory in March of 1991. Rangers went into the game on a 7-match unbeaten run and started well, Czech goalkeeper Jan Stejskal demonstrating the team's confidence with a smart save from Ian Rush in the opening

period. From that point on Rangers took a foothold in the game with Andy Sinton first forcing Mike Hooper into a save before taking the lead through Les Ferdinand, who headed-in from close range. Liverpool, clearly missing the influential John Barnes who was struck with 'flu, found themselves two down before the break when Wegerle pounced on a loose back-pass from David Burrows and rounded the keeper to score. Liverpool made changes to their defence in the second half and got themselves back into the game when Jan Molby converted a penalty kick after hand ball was given against Rangers defender Rufus Brevett. The goal galvanised Kenny Dalglish's team and they went close to getting an equaliser on a number of occasions, with Peter Beardsley hitting the post and Stejskal clawing away a header from Glenn Hysen. Just when it looked like Liverpool's relentless pressure would force an equaliser, the home crowd were stunned by a third Rangers goal. A Ferdinand cross was too high for Ray Wilkins and missed by Steve Nicol, but substitute Clive Wilson was there to stab the ball home and crown a memorable victory for the Rs.

QPR team: Stejskal, Bardsley, Brevett, Tilson, Peacock, Maddix, Wilkins, Barker, Ferdinand, Wegerle (Allen), Sinton (Wilson)

Manchester United 1–4 QPR
1 January 1992, First Division
When ITV decided to screen the New Year's Day clash between championship chasers Man United and QPR, few could have expected what was about to unfold in front of them as QPR recorded one their most famous victories. It was United's heaviest defeat at Old Trafford since losing 4–0 to Northampton in December 1978 and a result not bettered by any side in the modern United conquering era. Andy Sinton put the Rs ahead before Dennis Bailey raced through to make it 2–0 to Rangers with just 5 minutes on the clock. In the second half Bailey added his second, chipping Peter Schmeichel from the edge of the box and then completed his hat-trick when Sinton's shot cannoned off the post into his path for a simple

tap-in. United did nick a goal back but it didn't matter – the day belonged to Rangers and Bailey, who 19 years on remains the last English player to score a hat-trick at Old Trafford.

QPR team: Stejskal, Bardsley, Wilson, Wilkins, Peacock, McDonald, Holloway, Barker, Bailey, Wegerle, Sinton

Sheffield Wednesday 1–3 QPR
24 May 2004, Second Division

After missing out on promotion in the play-offs in 2003, Rangers endured a memorable up and down season the following year culminating in a trip to Hillsborough where a win would guarantee runners-up spot. Manager Ian Holloway named the same side for the third game in a row and the team flew out the traps, wasting early chances to take the lead through Marc Bircham and Paul Furlong. Wednesday countered and created some openings of their own until the Rangers breakthrough finally came just after the half-hour mark. Gareth Ainsworth sent a trademark ball into the box that was blocked by the defender only for it to fall to Kevin Gallen, who rammed the ball high into the net to send the Rangers fans crazy. Two minutes after the break it got even better for the Rs when Bircham picked out Furlong on the edge of the box and the veteran striker killed the ball on his chest, rolled it past Chris Carr and slotted in number two. Never ones to do things the easy way, Wednesday pulled one back on 59 when Jon Shaw drilled a low finish past Lee Camp. However, just as an equaliser looked likely Rangers got a slice of luck, when Martin Rowlands' low cross was turned into his own net by Carr to hand QPR the game. The final whistle brought scenes of jubilation from fans and players as promotion back the second tier was confirmed.

QPR team: Camp, Edghill, Carlisle (Gnohere), Rose, Padula, Ainsworth, Rowlands (Cureton), Bircham, Johnson, Furlong, Gallen

Watford 0–2 QPR
30 April 2011, Championship

In just a year at the helm at Loftus Road, Neil Warnock had put together a QPR side that had led the Championship table for all but two weeks of the season, and went into the game at Vicarage Road needing a win to secure promotion back to the Premier League. QPR's form had stuttered over the final weeks of the campaign and faced a Watford side that had already beaten them convincingly earlier that season. The visiting side made an enterprising start and Helguson saw a header saved by Scott Loach as QPR looked for the early goal. Watford, though, had chances of their own, going close through Lloyd Doyley and Danny Graham but the game remained goalless at the break. The second half saw much of the same pattern with both teams threatening goal, until Adel Taarabt sprung to life in the closing stages, meeting Tommy Smith's cross with 13 minutes to go to give Rangers the lead and send the away end into raptures. With the clock counting down on a memorable season, former Watford player Smith took the ball just outside the box and calmly placed a shot past Loach to seal the points and Rangers' return to the Premier League.

QPR team: Kenny, Orr, Hall (Shittu), Gorkss, Connolly, Derry, Taarabt (Ramage), Faurlin, Routledge (Buzsaky), Helguson, Smith

TESTIMONIALS

Something you seldom see in modern-day football is testimonial matches; games organised in honour of players who have contributed to a club over a substantial period of time. Rangers competed in and hosted a number of testimonials and benefit matches over the years, here's a complete list of the games staged.

22 April 1937	Brentford	H	for Dicky March
5 May 1938	Anglo-Scots	H	for Walter Barrie
13 April 1953	Ernie Adams XI	H	for Ernie Adams
29 March 1954	Manchester United	H	for Reg Allen
4 April 1955	All Stars XI	H	Players' benefit
17 October 1955	Portsmouth	H	Players' benefit
5 March 1956	All Star Managers XI	H	Players' benefit
24 March 1958	Showbiz XI	H	for Peter Angell and George Petchey
27 October 1958	All Star XI	H	Players' benefit
4 November 1959	Showbiz XI v Managers XI	H	Players' benefit
14 March 1960	Middlesex Wanderers	H	Players' benefit
20 May 1963	International XI v Showbiz XI	H	for Alec Farmer
3 May 1967	International XI	H	for Tony Ingham
7 May 1967	Ex-Brentford	A	for Tony Ingham
13 May 1968	Chelsea	H	for Mike Keen
14 May 1968	Wycombe Wanderers	A	for Mike Keen
3 May 1971	London XI	H	for Les Allen
5 May 1972	The Gazette Cup	H	for Frank Sibley
12 December 1972	Manchester City	H	for Frank Sibley
3 May 1974	Crystal Palace	H	for Ron Hunt
2 February 1976	Red Star Belgrade	H	for Mick Leach
10 March 1976	Watford	A	for Ian Morgan
10 August 1977	Wimbledon	A	for Dave Clement
13 August 1977	Wycombe Wanderers	A	for Dave Clement

5 May 1978	Manchester United	H	for Dave Clement
24 April 1979	Tottenham Hotspur	H	for Ian Gillard
29 April 1979	Burnham	A	for Ian Gillard
17 May 1982	Dave Clement XI	H	for Dave Clement
4 May 1983	Wimbledon	A	for Steve Jones and Tony Tagg
15 May 1987	Brentford	A	for Stan Bowles
15 February 1988	Charleroi	H	for Gary Waddock
11 May 1990	Chelsea	H	for Alan McDonald
22 April 1992	QPR Select XI	H	for Mick Leach
22 March 1998	Jamaica	H	for Simon Barker
5 May 2000	Tottenham Hotspur	H	for Danny Maddix
20 May 2003	Chelsea	H	for Gavin Peacock
4 August 2003	Charlton Athletic	H	for Tony Roberts
30 July 2005	Birmingham City	H	for Kevin Gallen

MOVES TO MERGE – II

Another West London merger was mooted during the 1986/87 season, this time with Fulham. Jim Gregory had finally found a buyer for his controlling stake in the club and in February 1987 sold out to Marler Estates, who were run by David Bulstrode and already owned Fulham. Due to Marler being a property company it was announced that that they had plans to merge the two clubs and play at Loftus Road. This would enable Marler to develop Craven Cottage into a housing estate in a prime London location. Fans voiced their opposition to the new 'Fulham Park Rangers' with a pitch invasion during the home game with Manchester City and due to the overwhelming opposition the idea was reduced to just a ground-sharing arrangement. David Bulstrode then changed the plans when he personally acquired Rangers from Marler and quashed all talk of mergers and ground shares. Thus both sides were able to keep their own identities and grounds.

ODD JOB MAN

Before playing for QPR, striker Les Ferdinand worked as a delivery driver, van steam cleaner and a plasterer's mate.

STRESS TEST

In June 2004, QPR manager Ian Holloway took part in a BBC television series called *Stress Test*. The documentary told the story of Holloway's fits of anger and how his temperament affected his life on and off the pitch as a football manager and father of three. Psychologists and consultants in anger management were involved in the programme which gave a unique insight to a side of footballers' lives not often seen by fans. Holloway later commented on the show, 'If I hadn't done that show, I wouldn't be sitting here now. Before I did it, I believed that I was a person who was kind, considerate and believed in free speech. The anger-management expert showed me I was a jumped-up, obnoxious little git who wouldn't listen at home because of what happened at work. If I'd carried on the way I was, I would have destroyed everything I ever had.'

SONG WARS

Before the 2003 Division Two play-off final between QPR and Cardiff City, a row erupted over what song should be played before kick-off, due to the English league game being held at the Millennium Stadium in Cardiff. Eventually neither 'God Save the Queen' nor 'Hen Wlad Fy Nhadau' were played and the clubs chose their own songs instead. Cardiff opted for 'Men of Harlech', while QPR went for their familiar anthem 'Papa's Got a Brand New Pigbag'.

INTERNATIONAL FIRSTS

Queens Park Rangers' first international player was Neal Murphy, who was selected to play for Ireland against England in February 1905. The centre forward who played for Rangers from 1903 until 1907 earned three caps for his country, scoring once, in the 2–2 draw with Wales in April 1905. A year later, Evelyn Lintott became the first QPR player to be selected for England when he was selected to play against Ireland in February 1908. It would be another 64 years before another Rangers player put on the Three Lions shirt, when Rodney Marsh was called up to play against Switzerland in November 1971.

SHARE AND SHARE ALIKE

QPR may have had more league grounds than any other club but they have also been kind enough to share their Loftus Road stadium on two occasions. In 2002, Rangers agreed to a ground share with local rivals Fulham, while Fulham's own home Craven Cottage was being redeveloped. The Cottagers spent two seasons at Loftus Road from 2002 to 2004, gaining averages of 16,707 and 16,342 in two successful Premier League campaigns. Fulham were preceded by rugby league side Wasps who, as part of Chris Wright-owned Loftus Road holdings, became London Wasps and shared the West London stadium from 1996 until 2002. The club even painted a wasp (the club emblem) into the Ellerslie Road stand for the duration of their stay, in which they won two RFU Cups.

FROM THE STANDS

There's never normally a dull moment among the fans on matchday at Loftus Road, with a whole catalogue of Rangers songs. These little ditties are reserved especially for some of the Rs' terrace favourites.

Chim chiminey, chim chiminey, chim chim cheroo,
who needs Sol Campbell when we've got Shittu?

Kevin Gallen's magic, he wears a magic hat
Kevin Gallen's magic, he's such a lovley chap
He scores with his left foot, he scores with his right
And when he plays against Chelsea, he scores all f***king night

We love you Bircham, 'cos you've got blue hair
We love you Bircham, 'cos you're everywhere
We love you Bircham, 'cos you're Rangers through and through

Shaun Derry, my lord, Shaun Derry
Shaun Derry, my lord, Shaun Derry
Oh lord, Shaun Derry

Saw my mate the other day, said to me we've signed the white Pele
Said to him, what's his name? Said to me, he's name Buzsaky
Buzsaky, Buzsaky, said to me he's name Buzsaky

RECORD-BREAKERS

Record Attendance
League – 35,353 v Leeds United, Division One, 27 April 1974
FA Cup – 41,097 v Leeds United, round three, 9 January 1932
League Cup – 28,739 v Aston Villa, semi-final, 1 February 1977

Record Margin of Victory
League (home) 9–2 v Tranmere Rovers, Division Three,
    3 December 1960
League (away) 7–1 Mansfield Town, Division Three,
    24 September 1966
FA Cup (home) 7–0 v Barry Town, round one,
    6 November 1961
FA Cup (away) 8–1 v Bristol Rovers, round one,
    27 November 1937
League Cup (home) 8–1 v Crewe Alexandra, round two,
    3 October 1983
League Cup (away) 5–1 Hull City, round two, 8 October 1985

Record Margin of Defeat
League (home) 0–5 v Burnley, Division Two, 21 January 1950
League (away) 1–8 v Mansfield Town, Division Three,
    15 March 1965
    1–8 v Manchester United, Division One, 19 March 1969
FA Cup (home) 0–6 v Arsenal, round four, 27 January 2001
FA Cup (away) 1–6 v Burnley, round three, 6 January 1962
    1–6 v Hereford United, round two, 7 December 1957

Most points in a season
(2 for a win) 67, Division Three 1966/67
(3 for a win) 85, Division Two 1982/83

Fewest points in a season
(2 for a win) 18, Division One 1968/69
(3 for a win) 33, Premier League 1995/96

Most Goals in a Season by Club
111– Division 3 (1961/62)

Most Goals in a Season by Player
44 – Rodney Marsh (1966/67)

Most League Goals in a Career
172 – George Goddard (1926–34)

Most League Appearances Made
519 – Tony Ingham (1950–63)

Most Capped International
52 – Alan McDonald, Northern Ireland

Record Transfer Fee Paid
£4.5 million – Anton Ferdinand from Sunderland, August 2011*
£3.5 million – Alejandro Faurlin from Instituto Atlético
    Central Córdoba, July 2009

Record Transfer Fee Received
£6 million – Les Ferdinand to Newcastle United, June 1995

Youngest Player
Frank Sibley 15 years 275 days

Oldest Player
Ray Wilkins 39 years 352 days

Best League run undefeated
20 from 3 December 1971 – 11 March 1972

Undefeated League home games
25 from 2 December 1972 – 12 April 1974

Undefeated League away games
17 from 10 September 1966 – 11 April 1967

Best run of League wins
8 from 7 November 1931 – 2 January 1932

*Speculated fee due to transfer being undisclosed

Best run of home League wins
11 from 26 December 1972 – 25 August 1973

Most clean sheets in one season
23, 2010/11

1976 AND ALL THAT ...

The 1975/76 season remains Queens Park Rangers' best ever season in the top flight of English football, finishing just a point behind Liverpool as runners-up in Division One. This is a month-by-month summary of that memorable campaign.

August
Rangers enjoyed a successful pre-season campaign that saw them defeat the champions of both West Germany and Portugal (Borussia Mönchengladbach and Benfica) and were in confident mood as they kicked off the season against previous campaign runners-up Liverpool. No Rangers side had ever beaten the Reds, but 27,000 fans were present to see QPR record their first ever win over the Merseysiders, as goals from Gerry Francis and Mick Leach secured a stylish opening-day victory. Three days later Francis was on the mark again as Rangers drew 1–1 with Aston Villa at Loftus Road. The following Saturday Rangers travelled to the Baseball Ground to face reigning champions Derby County and blew them away 5–1, with Stan Bowles netting a hat-trick. The month ended with draws with Wolverhampton Wanderers (2–2) and London rivals West Ham United (1–1).

September
The month began with Gerry Francis becoming the first Rangers player to be named England captain, when Don Revie gave the midfielder the armband for England's game against Switzerland in Basel. QPR continued their fine start to the

season with another unbeaten month, starting with a 1–1 win over Birmingham City at St Andrews. A packed Loftus Road then witnessed a 1–0 win over Manchester United thanks to Dave Webb's goal, before a goalless draw away at Middlesbrough. A week later Mick Leach's winner over Leicester City moved QPR to the top of First Division for the first time in the club's history. The Rs finished the month with another 1–0 win, this time against Newcastle United.

October

QPR's unbeaten run came to end at the start of October, when Leeds United beat Rangers 2–1 at Elland Road. Dave Sexton's men bounced back a week later, though, thrashing Everton with a 5-goal salvo that saw Gerry Francis (2), Don Givens, Don Masson and Dave Thomas on the score sheet. A 1–0 loss to Burnley briefly toppled Rangers from top-spot but October ended with a 1–0 win over Sheffield United and the club still top of the table.

November

Rangers greeted November with three successive draws against Coventry City (1–1), Tottenham Hotspur (0–0) and Ipswich Town (1–1) with Don Givens netting both goals. The Rs then gained revenge for the defeat at Turf Moor with a 1–0 win over Burnley thanks to a Stan Bowles winner. In the last game of the month, QPR came back from 2–1 down to beat Stoke City 3–2 and end November in second place, with just 6 points separating the top ten places.

December

After a goalless draw with Manchester City at Maine Road, 1975's end brought a tricky run of fixtures for Rangers, as they met fellow championship chasers Derby County and Liverpool. The Rams travelled to Loftus Road to face a crowd of over 25,000, and they looked to be going home happy when 17-year-old Phil Nutt headed in an 81st minute goal but Derby equalised through Bruce Rioch with the last kick of the game. The trip to Anfield on the 20th followed, where despite a spirited display Rangers suffered a 2–0 loss as goals from John Toshack and Phil Neal saw them fall to fourth in the table. A 2–0 win over Norwich City followed but Rangers slipped from the top four thanks to a 2–0 defeat to Arsenal in the last game of the year.

January

Rangers' first game of the New Year came 10 days in with a trip to Old Trafford, which ended in a 2–1 defeat for Dave Sexton's team. The lowest home gate of the season, just 16,700, turned up for the following fixture against relegation-threatened Birmingham City. Two goals from Don Masson gave Rangers a scrappy 2–1 win but a week later the 1–0 defeat to West Ham United started to provoke questions about the club's championship credentials. Rangers needed an instant reply and saved their best performance of the month for the 2–0 win at Villa Park that saw John Hollins score his first ever goal for the club.

February

Wolverhampton Wanderers travelled to W12 on the 7th for an action-packed game that featured a brace for Don Givens which, together with a penalty from Gerry Francis and a Dave Thomas goal, gave QPR a 4–2 win. A week later it was Francis' turn to net a double as his goals along with a Don Givens strike saw the Rs record a 3–0 win at White Hart Lane. Further wins over Ipswich Town (3–1) and Leicester City (1–0) and a point at Bramall Lane was enough to push Rangers right back into the title picture and level on points with leaders Liverpool at the top of the table.

March

QPR's rich vein of form continued into March, with goals from Dave Thomas, Gerry Francis, Don Givens and Don Masson giving the Rs a 4–1 win over Coventry City. A week later Stan Bowles and Mick Leach scored to gain a 2–0 win over Everton at Goodison Park, before Dave Webb netted winners in successive games against Stoke City and Manchester City to put QPR a point clear at the top of Division One as the season headed into its final month.

April

Back-to-back victories over Newcastle United (2–1) and Middlesbrough (4–2) meant Rangers were on a run of 6 straight wins and had won 11 of their last 12 matches. With three games to play Rangers led the table, a point clear of Liverpool and five clear of third-placed Manchester United. Victory in all three remaining matches would see the club crowned league champions for the first time. The first of those games was at Carrow Road to face Norwich City, but despite an own goal through Tony Powell and Dave Thomas' effort, the home side ran out 3–2 winners, as Liverpool beat Stoke 5–3.

Two days later a Frank McLintock goal and a Gerry Francis penalty was enough to see off Arsenal but Liverpool matched the Rs' result with a 3–0 win over Manchester City. It meant that QPR would need to beat Leeds United on the last day and hope the Reds would slip up against Wolverhampton Wanderers in their final fixture 10 days later. The game against Leeds attracted the biggest Loftus Road crowd of the season and goals from Dave Thomas and Stan Bowles meant Rangers had done all they could to secure the championship. Liverpool travelled to Molineux over a week later, with the hosts needing a win to stay in the division. Wolves held onto a 1–0 lead for 76 minutes before Kevin Keegan levelled and further goals from John Toshack and Ray Kennedy saw the title slip from Rangers' grasp and into the hands of the Merseyside giants once again. QPR finished the season by taking 27 points from a possible 30, but it wasn't enough and arguably the club's greatest ever side were denied a title their football and their season thoroughly deserved.

The final table, 4 May 1976:

		P	W	D	L	F	A	Gd	Pts
1	Liverpool	42	23	14	5	66	31	35	60
2	QPR	42	24	11	7	67	33	34	59
3	Man Utd	42	23	10	9	68	42	26	56
4	Derby Cty	42	21	11	10	75	58	17	53
5	Leeds Utd	42	21	9	12	65	46	19	51
6	Ipswich T	42	16	14	12	54	48	6	46
7	Leicester C	42	13	19	10	48	51	-3	45
8	Manchester C	42	16	11	15	64	46	18	43
9	Tottenham H	42	14	15	13	63	63	0	43
10	Norwich C	42	16	10	16	58	58	0	42
11	Everton	42	15	12	15	60	66	-6	42
12	Stoke C	42	15	11	16	48	50	-2	41
13	Middlesbrough	42	15	10	17	46	45	1	40
14	Coventry C	42	13	14	15	47	57	-10	40
15	Newcastle Utd	42	15	9	18	71	62	9	39
16	Aston Villa	42	11	17	14	51	59	-6	39
17	Arsenal	42	13	10	19	47	53	-6	36
18	West Ham Utd	42	13	10	19	48	71	-23	36
19	Birmingham C	42	13	7	22	57	75	-18	33
20	Wolves	42	10	10	22	51	68	-17	30
21	Burnley	42	9	10	23	43	66	-23	28
22	Sheffield Utd	42	6	10	26	33	82	-49	22

EUROPEAN RECORD

QPR have twice competed in the UEFA Cup, thanks to their second-place finish in 1976 and fifth-place finish in 1985. Here is the club's complete record in European competition.

1976/77
15 September 1976
Round one, first leg, QPR 4–0 Brann Bergen (H),
    Bowles (3), Masson
Team: Parkes, Clement, Gillard, Hollins, McLintock, Webb, Thomas, Leach, Masson, Bowles, Givens

29 September 1976
Round one, second leg, Brann Bergen 0–7 QPR (A),
    Bowles (3), Givens (2), Thomas, Webb
Team: Parkes, Clement, Gillard, Hollins, McLintock, Webb, Thomas, Leach (Busby), Masson, Bowles, Givens

20 October 1976
Round two, first leg, Slovan Bratislava 3–3 QPR(A),
    Bowles (2), Givens
Team: Parkes, Clement, Gillard, Hollins, McLintock, Webb, Thomas, Leach, Masson, Bowles, Givens

3 November 1976
Round two, second leg, QPR 5–2 Slovan Bratislava (H),
    Givens (3), Bowles, Clement
Team: Parkes, Clement, Gillard, Hollins, McLintock, Webb, Thomas, Leach, Masson, Bowles, Givens

24 November 1976
Round three, first leg, QPR 3–0 FC Cologne (H),
    Givens, Webb, Bowles
Team: Parkes, Clement, Gillard, Hollins, McLintock, Webb, Thomas, Leach, Masson, Bowles, Givens

7 December 1976
Round three, second leg, FC Cologne 4–1 QPR (A), Masson
Team: Parkes, Clement, Gillard, Hollins, McLintock, Webb, Thomas, Leach (Eastoe), Masson, Bowles, Givens

2 March 1977
Quarter-final, first leg, QPR 3–0 AEK Athens (H),
    Francis (2), Bowles
Team: Parkes, Kelly, Gillard, Hollins, McLintock, Webb, Thomas, Francis, Masson, Bowles, Givens

16 March 1977
Quarter-final, second leg, QPR 0–3 v AEK Athens (A)
Team: Parkes, Shanks, Gillard, Hollins, McLintock, Webb, Eastoe, Kelly, Masson, Bowles, Givens
(QPR lost on penalties)

1984–85
18 September 1984
Round one, first leg, KR Reykjavik 0–3 QPR (A),
    Stainrod (2), Bannister
Team: Hucker, Neil, Dawes, Fereday (Stewart), Wicks, Fenwick, Micklewhite, Fillery, Bannister (Charles), Stainrod, Gregory

2 October 1984
Round one, second leg, QPR 4–0 KR Reykjavik (H),
    Bannister (3), Charles
Team: Hucker, Neil (Allen), Dawes, Fereday, Wicks, Fenwick, Stewart, Fillery (Cooper), Bannister, Charles, Gregory

24 October 1984
Round two, first leg, QPR 6–2 Partizan Belgrade (H),
    Gregory, Fereday, Neil, Stainrod, Bannister (2)
Team: Hucker, Neil, Dawes, Fereday, Wicks, Fenwick, Stewart (Burke), Fillery, Bannister, Stainrod, Gregory

7 November 1984
Round two, second leg, Partizan Belgrade 4–0 QPR (A)
Team: Hucker, Chivers, Dawes, Fereday, Wicks, Fenwick, Waddock (Micklewhite), Fillery, Bannister, Stainrod, Gregory
(QPR lost on away goals)

FIVE (NOT SO) GREAT GAMES

Manchester United 8–1 QPR
19 March 1969 First Division
This was the day Rangers suffered their heaviest ever defeat as United, led by the mercurial George Best and deadly Denis Law, ran riot at Old Trafford. Incredibly Rangers held their own for the majority of the first half, with young goalkeeper Alan Spratley keeping the Rs in the game with a string of impressive stops. However, he could only keep United's talented side at bay for so long and just before the half-hour Willie Morgan nodded the opening goal off a Best corner. In the second half United took full control and two further strikes from Morgan, a brace by Best and goals from Nobby Stiles, Brian Kidd and John Aston gave the Red Devils a massive 8-goal haul. Rodney Marsh did net a consolation goal but it would go down as the club's record defeat in a season that would see QPR finish bottom and relegated to the Second Division.

QPR team: Spratley, Watson, Clement, Hazell, Hunt, Sibley, I. Morgan, Leach, Clarke, Marsh, Glover

Norwich City 3–2 QPR
17 April 1976 First Division
Carrow Road is still regarded as a place of melancholy by QPR fans, thanks to this defeat that knocked the club off the top of the table and ended their championship challenge. In a game played at cup tie pace, it was Norwich who dealt the

first blow when Ted McDougall opened the scoring in the 27th minute, only for Dave Clement to level the scores at the break. Rangers, who were unbeaten in 13 matches going into the game, were still favourites for the win but City, buoyed by their biggest crowd of the season, netted twice in the second half through John Morris. Dave Sexton's team rallied and forced the home side into conceding an own goal through Powell, but it wasn't enough and the defeat gave Liverpool an advantage in the title race they never let slip. Rangers did end the season with two wins over Arsenal and Leeds United but finished a point behind the Merseysiders and have yet to ever go as close to a title win again.

QPR team: Parkes, Clement, Gillard, Hollins, McLintock, Webb, Thomas, Francis, Masson, Bowles, Givens

Oxford United 3–0 QPR
20 April 1986 Milk Cup final

Jim Smith's Queens Park Rangers went into this Wembley final against Oxford United as strong favourites having already beaten United that season and disposing of Liverpool in the semi-final. However, Oxford managed to record one of the competition's most comfortable final victories with a 3-goal salvo under the Twin Towers. Oxford took the lead just before the break with a simple goal laid on by John Aldridge and scored by Trevor Hebberd. From that point they never looked back with Rangers scarcely carving out any openings. Their fate was sealed on 52 minutes when Ray Houghton finished off a neat one-two with Hebberd to effectively put the game to bed and hand the Us the trophy. Rangers turned in a desperately disappointing performance and didn't even record a shot on target until the 72nd minute. Their misery was completed when Jeremy Charles added a third for Oxford with four minutes left.

QPR team: Barron, McDonald, Dawes, Neil, Wicks, Fenwick, Allen (Rosenior), James, Bannister, Byrne, Robinson

QPR 1–1 Vauxhall Motors (QPR lost 3–4 on penalties)
26 November 2002 FA Cup first round replay

This was perhaps Rangers' lowest ebb of the modern era, and certainly one of their most embarrassing results, as non-league Vauxhall Motors dumped them out of the FA Cup. It got off to a bright enough start and Rangers opened the scoring on 18 minutes when Gino Padula picked out Andy Thomson with a low pass that Thomson dinked over the advancing keeper. That should have been the impetus for Rangers to go on and win the game comfortably but the plucky part-timers fought their way back into the game with some quite delightful football. Skipper Phil Brazier equalised just 4 minutes later and they continued with wave after wave of attack on the Rangers goal. The second half bought more chances for both sides with Rangers squandering a number of openings and Motors forcing Fraser Digby into saves at the other end. The game went into extra-time but still the sides could not be separated and it went down to penalties. Paul Furlong missed Rangers' first, giving Motors the advantage – and one they took by converting all four of their spot-kicks. It meant Karl Connolly had to score to keep Rangers in it, but his effort missed the target and the team from Cheshire recorded a famous victory over Second Division QPR.

QPR team: Digby, Forbes, Palmer, Carlisle, Padula (Connolly), Burgess, Bircham, Langley, Williams (Murphy), Thomson, Furlong

Cardiff City 1–0 QPR
25 May 2003 Second Division play-off final

After a miserable period at the beginning of the millennium, Rangers under Ian Holloway were a team on the up and reached the play-off final in 2003 hoping to book their return back to the second tier of English football. The game was controversially played in Cardiff due to building work on the new Wembley Stadium giving QPR's opponents a distinct advantage in the Welsh capital's 60,000-seater stadium. Rangers donned an all-white strip in a bid to invoke memories of the 1967 FA Cup-winning side but the game turned out to be a tight contest with very few chances. The best of the action came in extra time when Tommy Williams found himself with space to square the ball to a waiting Paul Furlong but instead opted to shoot and the ball blazed over the bar. Minutes later Rangers were left to rue that missed opportunity as Andy Campbell came off the Bluebirds bench to net the game's winner with just 6 minutes left and condemn Rangers to a further season in Division Two.

QPR team: Day, Kelly, Carlisle, Shittu, Padula (Williams), Gallen, Palmer, Bircham, McLeod, Pacquette (Thomson), Furlong

TAXI!

On 4 April 1963, QPR's Loftus Road ground hosted an unusual international match, when taxi drivers from England and Scotland met to compete in the Bell Punch Taximeter Challenge Cup. The annual event, which first began in 1929, saw England represented by the Mocatre London Taxi FC play Scotland's Edinburgh and Glasgow Taxi Drivers FC.

LOFTUS ROAD LEGEND – DAVE THOMAS

In a career spanning 20 years and six clubs, winger Dave Thomas is best remembered for his time at Loftus Road. Born and raised in Nottingham, Thomas signed pro forms with Burnley at 16 and was tipped as a future England international. He was fast-tracked to the first team and made his debut on the last day of the 1966/67 season against Everton. In turn, at 16 years and 220 days he became the second youngest player ever to play for the club after Tommy Lawton.

Within two years he'd become a first-team regular but couldn't stop the club from being relegated to the Second Division.

Thomas stayed with the Clarets the following campaign and played in all but five of Burnley's games. Speculation began to mount that Thomas would be moving on, but it was a surprise when Burnley sold him to promotion rivals QPR in October 1972. Thomas, a right-winger, was brought in to replace the injured Martyn Busby who was a left-winger and at first Thomas struggled to adapt to the new position. Once acclimatised, though, he would go on to excel in his new role and become a huge fan favourite at Loftus Road with his mazy runs and ability to get skip past defenders. Thomas helped Rangers to promotion in his first season (ironically alongside Burnley) and over his four years in Shepherd's Bush he was an integral part of what was arguably Rangers' greatest ever team, coming within a whisker of winning the league title in 1976. He also won eight England caps in his time with Rangers. Thomas left the Super Hoops a year later, joining Everton before enjoying spells with Wolverhampton Wanderers, Middlesbrough, Portsmouth and Vancouver Whitecaps.

DID YOU KNOW?

After retiring from football, Dave Thomas became a PE teacher at Bishop Luffa School in Chichester.

NAME GAME

Former Brighton & Hove Albion and Torquay United midfielder Charlie Oatway may have never played for QPR but he holds a unique association with the club. Both Oatway's parents were huge QPR fans and actually named their son after the entire 1973 Rangers squad. His real full name is Anthony Philip David Terry Frank Donald Stanley Gerry Gordon Stephen James Oatway. When his parents told his aunt the proposed name, she said 'he'd look a right Charlie,' and the name stuck.

TWITTER

One of football's most modern ways of communicating is through the social networking site Twitter. The site gives fans, journalists and players the opportunity to keep in touch via 140-character messages and counts a number of former and current QPR players as members, including:

Current playing and coaching staff

Adel Taarabt	@adeltaarabt
Hogan Emphraim	@HoganEphraim
Jay Bothroyd	@jaybothroyd
DJ Campbell	@RealDJCampbell
Kieron Dyer	@KieronDyer8
Shaun Derry	@greypeacock
Paddy Kenny	@PatrickKenny1978
Bradley Orr	@bradleyorr2
Alejandro Faurlin	@alefaurlin
Jamie Mackie	@jamiemac12
Clint Hill	@clinthill3
Fitz Hall	@aslfitzhall
Danny Shittu	@danshittu
Rowan Vine	@aslrowanvine
Peter Ramage	@peterramage83
Michael Doughty	@mdoughty92
Joey Barton	@Joey7Barton
Shaun Wright-Phillips	@swp29
Jason Puncheon	@jasonpunch
Michael Harriman	@Mharriman40
Anton Ferdinand	@anton_ferdinand
Bruno Andrade	@brunsky36
Brian Murphy	@b_murphy01gk
Keith Curle	@keithcurle23
Marc Bircham	@marcbircham

Current board members

Tony Fernandes	@tonyfernandes
Amit Bhatia	@Amit_Bhatia99
Philip Beard	@philipb1

Former Rs

Rodney Marsh	@RodneyMarsh10
Rufus Brevett	@RufusBrevett3
Richard Langely	@LANGERS1979
Ismael Miller	@IshmaelMiller
Mikele Leigertwood	@ALSmleigertwood
Wayne Routledge	@WayneRoutledge
Dexter Blackstock	@dexblackstock23
Zesh Rehman	@Zesh_Rehman
Daniele Dichio	@DannyDichio
Kaspars Gorkss	@EsUnPiens
Dave Seaman	@thedavidseaman
Andy Impey	@Aimpey
Rufus Brevett	@Rufusbrevett3
Warren Barton	@warrenbarton2

THE BADGES

The first badge to appear on a QPR shirt was in 1954 when, with the consent of Hammersmith Council, the borough's coat of arms was included on Rangers' first all-white home jerseys. The detailed coat of arms featured a number of elements related to the borough, including:

The two crosslets, azure and argent for Edward Latymer, a citizen of London who raised money for the poor of Hammersmith and established the Latymer Upper School for young boys.

The chevron and three horses for Sir Nicholas Crispe, who gave the bricks and funded the building of the Parish Church in Hammersmith.

An escallop shell and bridge for George Ping, a surgeon at Hammersmith and the projector of the suspension bridge that increased facilities and communication within the town.

Hammers, for the name Hammersmith.

In 1975 a first proper crest was introduced with a simple design that featured the initials QPR inside a white or blue football depending on what hoop it appeared on. Seven years on, the badge was updated with a design that would become the club's most famous logo. The initials remained but in a different more luxurious font, inside a blue circle. A second circle around the letters included the name Queens Park Rangers and the whole thing sat on a scroll, that would later include '1882', the year the club was formed, and the ground's name, Loftus Road.

The badge stayed that way until the arrival of Flavio Briatore and Bernie Eccelstone in 2007, who signalled their takeover and new era with a new crest for the club – much to the fans' disappointment. Gone were the intertwined initials and in their place a hooped shield, a crown and silver branches. The scroll remained with the word 'London' added alongside the ground and the year. The crest was unveiled in grand style with a host of QPR legends launching it at Loftus Road alongside fireworks, but it was not well received by the fans and became a symbol of the frustration aimed at the board during their controversial reign.

LOFTUS ROAD LEGEND – ALAN McDONALD

Joining Queens Park Rangers as a schoolboy, McDonald had to wait for his first chance of first-team football, and actually made his professional debut while on loan at Charlton Athletic during a 9-game spell at the Valley in 1983. However, the departure of Bob Hazell gave him the chance of first-team action for Rangers and he would become a permanent fixture in the QPR back line for the next decade.

During his 500-odd games with the Super Hoops, McDonald played under ten different managers and played in some memorable Rangers sides, including the 1986 League Cup final team, and was skipper of the Gerry Francis side that finished as the top London club in the inaugural Premier League season – forming great partnerships with Paul Parker, Danny Maddix and Darren Peacock along the way. McDonald gained international honours too, and made his debut for Northern Ireland in 1986, going on to win 52 caps and representing Northern Ireland at the 1986 World Cup – he is still QPR's most capped international. The low point, though, was seeing Rangers relegated from the Premier League, and although McDonald stayed for the following season vowing in vain to get the side back up, he was released by Stewart Houston in 1997 and joined Swindon Town. He only lasted one season as a player at Swindon, memorably keeping goal for the Robins at Loftus Road after a sending-off and keeping his former club out in a 1–0 win, before becoming the reserve team coach at the County Ground. In 2006 McDonald returned to his beloved Rangers as assistant manager to Gary Waddock – it wasn't to last long though, as a poor Rangers side soon saw the dismissal of Waddock and McDonald after just six months and John Gregory was brought in as manager. McDonald was named manager of IFA Premiership side Glentoran in 2007 but left the club after a 3-year spell and is now unofficially retired.

DID YOU KNOW?

After Northern Ireland's draw with England in 1986 was accused to have been a fix, Alan McDonald offered anybody who believed the story to meet him outside! Funnily enough no one did.

PAYING THE PENALTY

Rangers have competed in six penalty shoot-outs during their history, with a 50 per cent win record. Here are the six:

16 March 1977	UEFA Cup	v AEK Athens	L 3–4
3 September 1980	League Cup	v Derby County	W 5–3
14 February 1989	Simod Cup	v Watford	W 5–4
6 October 1992	League Cup	v Grimsby Town	W 6–5
25 August 1999	League Cup	v Cardiff City	L 2–3
26 November 2002	FA Cup	v Vauxhall Motors	L 4–5

SPORTS SWITCH

Before the start of the 1989/90 season, manager Trevor Francis brought back the Supporters' Club Open Day. On this occasion the afternoon featured a cricket match between the QPR first-team players and the hosts of the event Shepherd's Bush Cricket Club. The match ended in a 185–9 over 147 win for the 'home side' but some of the Rangers players' performances, including the bowling of David Seaman and Alan McDonald's exploits behind the stumps, caught the eye.

PERFECT START

The following is a list of all QPR players who have scored on their debut for the club.

9 October 1948	Stan Hudson	v Brentford
27 January 1951	Edmund Davies	v Brentford
17 March 1953	Conway Smith	v Leeds United
8 March 1952	Oscar Hold	v Southampton
18 October 1952	Gordon Quinn	v Newport County
8 November 1952	Derek Parsons	v Torquay United
28 February 1953	Ronald Higgins	v Brighton & Hove Albion
13 October 1956	Tesi Balogun	v Watford
15 December 1956	Terence Peacock	v Reading
16 March 1959	George Whitelaw	v Bradford City

17 September 1960	Mark Lazarus	v Colchester United
19 August 1961	Jim Towers	v Brentford
30 September 1961	George Francis	v Hull City
7 October 1961	John McClelland	v Newport County
24 August 1963	Malcolm Graham	v Oldham Athletic
25 September 1964	Billy McAdams	v Hull City
26 February 1965	Mick Leach	v Colchester United
27 December 1966	Alan Wilks	v Brighton & Hove Albion
24 August 1968	Barry Bridges	v Watford
17 October 1970	Andy McCulloch	v Birmingham City
16 September 1972	Stan Bowles	v Nottingham Forest
10 September 1973	Ron Abbott	v West Ham United
31 March 1979	Mickey Walsh	v Derby County
19 August 1980	Wayne Fereday	v Bristol Rovers
19 December 1980	Mike Flanagan	v Bolton Wanderers
25 April 1982	Ian Muir	v Cambridge United
15 August 1987	Kevin Brock	v West Ham United
11 March 1989	Colin Clarke	v Newcastle United
19 August 1989	Paul Wright	v Crystal Palace
17 August 1991	Dennis Bailey	v Arsenal
14 September 1996	Mark Perry	v Barnsley
23 November 1996	John Spencer	v Reading
5 April 1997	Steve Morrow	v Bolton Wanderers
28 March 1998	Vinnie Jones	v Huddersfield Town
4 November 2001	Paul Peschisolido	v Portsmouth
9 August 2003	Gareth Ainsworth	v Blackpool
3 October 2007	Rowan Vine	v Colchester United
7 August 2010	Jamie Mackie	v Barnsley

THE OWNERS

When Jim Gregory took over the club and became chairman in April 1965 it started a reign that would see him at the helm for an incredible 27 years. During that time he'd see Rangers progress from a Third Division club to one that celebrated League Cup glory in 1967, taste European football in the mid-1970s and establish themselves as a top-flight club.

In February 1987, Marler Estates bought the club with David Bulstrode appointed chairman. Bulstrode then took over the club outright before his death in September 1988 and Richard Thompson became chairman – becoming the Football League's youngest ever chairman in the process at just 24. Thompson's controversial spell lasted 8 years until the family sold the club to Chrysalis boss Chris Wright. But with Rangers' on-pitch exploits taking a downward turn and Wright unable to refinance the club, QPR went into administration in April 2001 and Wright left. A new board was brought in a year later by means of a £10 million loan but although former World Cup-winning captain Dunga headed up the consortium, the leaders were never really identified. Gianni Paladini became chairman in 2005 and with the club still not financially secure, he helped bring in F1 boss Bernie Ecclestone and Benetton owner Flavio Briatore who paid off the club's loan and acquired the vast majority of the shares. The pair later sold around 20 per cent to billionaire Lakshmi Mittal and the Mittal family, sparking stories of Rangers suddenly becoming one of the world's richest clubs. The Briatore and Ecclestone reign was a controversial one, with the pair changing the club's badge, raising ticket prices and hiring and firing managers on a whim. In the 2009/10 season alone, QPR saw five managers come and go. Upon QPR's promotion to the Premier League in 2011, the pair actively put the club up for sale and thus restricted boss Neil Warnock's funds for the forthcoming season. In August 2011, Lotus boss Tony Fernandes bought out Briatore and Ecclestone's shares to become majority shareholder and new company chairman.

LOFTUS ROAD LEGEND – PHIL PARKES

Les Allen swooped to bring in 6ft 3in stopper Phil Parkes in June 1970, paying Walsall just £15,000 for his services. He made his debut in a 2–1 home defeat to Leicester City at the beginning of the 1970/71 season and thus began a run of 109 consecutive games for the Rs. In fact Parkes only missed 2 games in his first 6 seasons at Loftus Road as part of the QPR side that won promotion to the First Division and then went a single point off taking the league title from Liverpool in the memorable 1975/76 campaign.

Parkes won 7 England U23 caps while at Rangers, but owing to playing in an era that included such top goalkeepers such as Peter Shilton, Ray Clemence and Joe Corrigan, only managed one full cap against Portugal in April 1975, keeping a clean sheet in the process.

After making 406 appearances for Rangers, Parkes moved to West Ham United in February 1979. The £565,000 fee received was a world record amount for a goalkeeper at the time and he went on to enjoy a successful spell at Upton Park, winning the FA Cup in his first season and being widely regarded as the club's best ever number 1. A brief spell at Ipswich followed before he went into coaching, returning to Loftus Road as goalkeeping coach in 1992 under Gerry Francis.

DID YOU KNOW?

In 1982 Phil Parkes appeared as himself in *Eagle*'s 'Thunderbolt and Smokey' comic strip, giving a coaching session to the boys' team.

FIVE (MORE) GREAT GOALS

Trevor Francis v Aston Villa
23 September 1989, First Division
Trevor Francis may have been in the twilight of his career in his time at Loftus Road, but he still showed glimpses of the talent that made him Britain's first million-pound player – including this real wonder goal. A long QPR throw-in was eventually headed out of the Villa penalty area, but only as far as Francis

on the left-hand edge of the box. With perfect poise and prowess, Francis flicked the ball up with one foot and volleyed it with other, then saw it loop over the Villa goalkeeper and into the far corner of the net.

Les Ferdinand v Manchester United
10 December 1994, Premier League
Les Ferdinand scored nearly 100 goals for QPR in his 9-year stint, but none better than a spectacular strike against then champions Manchester United back in Rangers' last Premier League era. After gaining possession from Trevor Sinclair 30 yards from goal, the Rs' number 9 – with his back to goal – fought off the challenge of Paul Ince before firing a wonderfully placed shot into the top corner, giving the great Peter Schmeichel no chance in front of the School End.

Daniele Dichio v Wolverhampton Wanderers
1 September 1996, First Division
Voted the division's Goal of the Season that year, it was strikes like this that ultimately persuaded Italian club Sampdoria to offer Dichio a contract at the end of that campaign. A long ball from defence was met by a deft header from Trevor Sinclair, that perfectly teed-up Dichio to unleash a thunderous volley giving the Wolves keeper no chance. From the celebration that followed you can tell he enjoyed that one too.

Gareth Ainsworth v Rushden and Diamonds
25 August 2003, Second Division
During a 7-year stay in W12, Gareth Ainsworth achieved cult status with the QPR faithful thanks to his never-say-die attitude, all-action displays and moments like this against Rushden and Diamonds. Kevin McLeod sprayed the ball across from the left flank where a raging Ainsworth met it on the volley from 25 yards out, crashing the ball into the roof of the net. It was preceded by an equally impressive strike for the winger on an afternoon that very much belonged to Rangers' 'wild thing'.

Wayne Routledge v Coventry

23 January 2011, Championship

A mark of a truly great championship-winning side is to have players who can win games with one moment of pure quality, such as this goal from QPR's promotion-winning campaign in 2011. With the game locked at 1–1, talisman Adel Taarabt collected the ball on the left wing. Spotting the run of team-mate Routledge, the Moroccan bent a pass with the outside of his right foot that split the Sky Blues defence open and fell perfectly into the path of Routledge, who controlled with one touch and flicked it past Keiren Westwood.

ONE-GAME WONDERS

Not all the players who have donned the blue and white hoops have managed to establish themselves as a permanent Rangers first-teamer. Some, like the following players, even hold the unfortunate honour of appearing for the club only once. The shortest QPR career belongs to Carl Leaburn whose spell in W12 was reduced to a 3-minute appearance against Reading in 2005.

John Cole	v Bristol Rovers	1/9/1900	SLD1
Dave Cowan	v Northampton	16/12/1905	SLD1
Walter Corbett	v New Brompton	7/9/1907	SLD1
Robert McEwan	v Southampton	26/12/1908	SLD1
W. Lowe	v Millwall	8/11/1919	SLD1
Albert Chester	v Brighton & HA	15/11/1919	SLD1
Charles Thompson	v Brentford	29/10/1921	D3S
Sidney Bailey	v Merthyr T	22/4/1922	D3S
James Leach	v Watford	26/8/1922	D3S
Robert Dand	v Norwich C	25/12/1924	D3S
William Drew	v Charlton A	18/9/1926	D3S
Alfred Bowers	v Bournemouth	2/10/1926	D3S
Eddie Beats	v Millwall	19/3/1928	D3S
William Goodman	v Norwich C	18/4/1928	D3S
Norman Crompton	v Norwich C	3/5/1928	D3S
Hugh Vallance	v Watford	16/2/1929	D3S

Ernie Wright	v Brighton & HA	26/1/1935	D3S
George Ives	v Watford	1/3/1938	D3S
Ronald Stevens	v Port Vale	4/5/1939	SC
Joe Millbank	v Barnsley	11/9/1948	D2
Peter Fallon	v Shrewsbury T	19/9/1953	D3S
Ian Allen	v Bournemouth	7/4/1954	D3S
Alan Silver	v Walthamstow	29/11/1954	FAC
George Dawson	v Colchester Utd	10/3/1956	D3S
Albert Allum	v Colchester Utd	2/9/1957	D3S
Paddy Hasty	v Wrexham	4/5/1960	D3
Rodney Slack	v Halifax T	3/4/1962	D3
George Jacks	v Exeter C	24/4/1965	D3
Andy Pape	v Charlton A	13/4/1980	D2
Graham Benstead	v WBA	8/1/1983	FAC
Martin Duffield	v Grimsby T	14/5/1983	D2
Kurt Bakholt	v Manchester C	8/2/1986	D1
Tony Witter	v Aston Villa	14/8/1993	PL
Ademola Bankole	v Tranmere R	9/10/1999	D1
Hamid Barr	v Yeovil T	16/10/2001	LDVVT
Justin Cochrane	v Stockport Cty	28/4/2001	D1
Alvin Bubb	v Wolves	6/5/2001	D1
Alex Higgins	v Wolves	6/5/2001	D1
Carl Leaburn	v Reading	5/1/2002	D2
Brian Fitzgerald	v Bury	12/1/2002	D2
Matt Hislop	v Leicester City	24/92005	Ch
Keith Lowe	v Leeds United	4/2/2006	Ch
Andrew Howell	v Northampton	22/8/2006	LC

SLD1 = Southern League Division One
D3S = Division Three South
D2 = Division Two
D1 = Division One
Ch = Championship
PL = Premier League
FAC = FA Cup
LC = League Cup
SC = Southern Cup
LDVVT = LD Vans Trophy

ROCK AND BOWLES

London rockers The Others have made no secret of their love for all things QPR and even recorded a song called 'Stan Bowles' on their 2005 debut album. The song reached number 36 in the UK singles chart and the band even performed the track live on BBC Radio One. The full lyrics to the track are:

When I first met you
You were wearing, wearing a tunic
Eyes glazed over, stripped right back like a hollow
We'd talk for days in a room off Cambridge Heath Road
Smoking bone in your backroom
While your sister, while your sister phoned
While your sister, while your sister phoned
While your sister, while your sister phoned
I'd stare at your eyes as you helped the children
You're quoting Voltaire or Ginsberg
To the adorned in your kitchen
Sipping ice tea in the summer
Picture a park, yeah

Playing at being Stan Bowles
QPR Nineteen seventy-five
QPR Nineteen seventy-five
QPR Nineteen seventy-five
QPR Nineteen seventy-five
QPR Nineteen seventy-five

Then you helped me out
You gave me a break, a break from the boredom
I quit my job
I took a gamble, a gamble on a new life
I'll always remember staying with you in your hotel
I'll always owe you son
Gratitude gratitude my friend
Gratitude gratitude my friend
Gratitude gratitude my friend
Gratitude gratitude my friend

AVERAGE ATTENDANCES

Queens Park Rangers have played in 91 competitive seasons as a professional club. The following are the crowd averages in descending order from the 1920/21 season. The list unsurprisingly demonstrates QPR's biggest boom period being in the mid-1970s as a championship chasing club, with the late 1940s also showing a strong period. Of the more modern all-seater era, 2011's promotion campaign is the highest attended, just above Rangers' 2005/06 return to the Championship.

Season	Attendance	Season	Attendance
1975/76	23,422	1920/21	14,409
1973/74	23,307	1979/80	14,365
1947/48	22,828	1994/95	14,360
1948/49	22,044	1993/94	13,856
1968/69	21,572	1937/38	13,799
1976/77	21,081	2003/04	13,766
1974/75	20,125	2008/09	13,640
1977/78	19,797	2007/08	13,596
1949/50	19,437	1986/87	13,574
1969/70	18,921	1928/29	13,487
1967/68	18,558	1989/90	13,471
1950/51	17,485	2005/06	13,441
1946/47	16,786	1966/67	13,392
1978/79	16,665	1984/85	13,386
1951/52	16,504	2009/10	13,349
2010/11	15,635	1987/88	13,233
2004/05	15,412	1990/91	13,178
1995/96	15,386	1970/71	13,042
1985/86	15,287	1981/82	12,912
1983/84	15,257	1997/98	12,906
1971/72	14,967	1991/92	12,769
1992/93	14,682	2002/03	12,734
1972/73	14,665	1982/83	12,663
1931/32	14,567	2006/07	12,487

1945/46	12,486	1924/25	9,943
1996/97	12,337	1926/27	9,706
1999/2000	12,183	1960/61	9,615
1988/89	12,124	1957/58	9,528
2000/01	12,066	1958/59	9,318
1952/53	12,046	1956/57	9,260
1938/39	11,930	1930/31	9,168
1980/81	11,727	1923/24	9,000
1922/23	11,672	1944/45	8,702
1921/22	11,610	1955/56	8,695
1953/54	11,544	1965/66	8,290
1929/30	11,535	1963/64	7,992
2001/02	11,470	1925/26	7,823
1954/55	11,426	1934/35	7,705
1998/99	11,374	1932/33	7,602
1935/36	11,113	1943/44	7,419
1961/62	10,991	1942/43	6,141
1959/60	10,588	1964/65	5,724
1936/37	10,552	1941/42	4,795
1933/34	10,281	1939/40	4,535
1962/63	10,222	1940/41	2,368
1927/28	10,115		

MOVES TO MERGE – III

In 2001 QPR came close to merging for a third time, when negotiations took place between Rangers and South London Premier League club Wimbledon. At the time the talks took place, QPR were in administration with debts of £8 million while Wimbledon were playing at Crystal Palace's Selhurst Park without a home of their own and in front of crowds of only a few thousand fans. The move on paper made financial sense and the wheels were put in motion to form the new club for the start of the 2001/02 season. With it leaked to the press and headlines such as 'Quimbledon' and 'Queens Park Dons' QPR released an official statement confirming the talks, that stated:

> It is true that we are in very early stage discussions with Wimbledon Football Club about a possible merger. It is not helpful that the news has leaked as we were intent on exploring the opportunity in a sensible and controlled manner which included sending a letter to all season ticket holders, club members, and shareholders asking them for their opinion and whether the proposal is worth pursuing. Should these discussions continue the questionnaires will be distributed in the near future and we welcome honest and constructive feedback. The talks with Wimbledon will only continue if there is general approval from our supporter base.
>
> Our initial view is that in the current financial environment for football outside the Premier League the idea could have merit and maybe worth exploring further but we must emphasise it is still very early days and no firm agreement whatsoever has been reached. Any merger will clearly be subject to the approval of the Football League, however the nature of the talks have included the possibility of the new club playing in Division One at Loftus Road, with the name and colours reflecting elements of both clubs.
>
> At this time there is little more that can be said until the views of our supporters have been canvassed and a decision is made as to whether to take discussions further or not.

Unsurprisingly there was vigorous opposition to the merger from both sets of supporters and only three days later the club released a second statement announcing the club had abandoned the merger. It read:

> After serious consideration and talks with supporters, the boards of Loftus Road and Queens Park Rangers have decided not to take discussions with Wimbledon Football Club regarding a possible merger, any further. Although the proposal had some financial and theoretical merit, the

strength of feeling from supporters to maintain the QPR identity and history was overwhelming, and had it gone ahead would have alienated, perhaps irrevocably, a large section of supporters without whom the club could not survive. Discussions, however, continue with other interested parties and the board, together with the administrators, are working hard to secure the best deal for the future of the club.

PAST IT?

Since 2000 the Masters events have been regularly held every summer and shown on Sky Sports. The event is held regionally, with the winners of every tournament going on to grand finals to compete for the Masters Grand Final Cup. QPR first took part in the event, which features over-35s, in 2005, and have since gone on to win the London finals on two occasions. Here's Rangers' complete record in the popular competition.

2005 – Southern Masters

Squad
Warren Neil
Kevin Brock
Andy Tillson
Steve Palmer
Gary Waddock
Karl Connolly
John Byrne
Dean Wilkins
Wayne Fereday

QPR 2–2 Spurs (Byrne, Tilson)
QPR 1–1 Arsenal (Byrne)
QPR 2–3 West Ham United (Byrne, Connolly)

2006 – London Masters

Squad
Tony Roberts
Danny Maddix
Andy Tillson
Steve Palmer
Michael Meaker
Maurice Doyle
John Byrne
Karl Connolly
Bradley Allen

QPR 4–4 Chelsea (Byrne, Meaker 2, Tillson)
QPR 2–1 West Ham United (Connolly, Doyle)
QPR 3–0 Southampton (Connolly, Byrne, Tillson)

Final
QPR 1–5 Chelsea (Meaker)

2009 – London Masters

Squad
Tony Roberts
Steve Palmer
Danny Maddix
Michael Meaker
Bradley Allen
Andy Tillson
Tony Thorpe
Karl Connolly
Andy Sinton

QPR 3–0 Fulham (Sinton, Meaker 2)
QPR 1–1 Chelsea (Sinton)

Final
QPR 1–1 West Ham United (Thorpe), QPR won 4–3 on penalties

2009 – Masters Grand Finals

Squad
Tony Roberts
Richard Edghill
Andy Tillson
Andy Sinton
Maurice Doyle
Karl Connolly
Michael Meaker
Bradley Allen
Tony Thorpe

Middlesbrough 5–2 QPR (Meaker, Thorpe)

2010 – London Masters

Squad
Simon Royce
Tim Breacker
Matthew Rose
Marcus Bignot
Wayne Fereday
Michael Meaker
Tony Thorpe
Karl Connolly

QPR 3–2 Tottenham Hotspur (Meaker, Bignot, Thorpe)
QPR 3–0 Arsenal (Bignot 3)

Final
QPR 3–3 West Ham United (Meaker 3), QPR won 4–2 on penalties

2010 – Masters Grand Finals

Squad
Simon Royce
Tim Breacker
Matthew Rose
Marcus Bignot
Wayne Fereday
Michael Meaker
Tony Thorpe
Karl Connolly

QPR 3–3 Barnsley (Bignot, Meaker, Thorpe) Barnsley won
4–2 on penalties

2011 – London Masters

Squad
Lee Harrison
Marcus Bignot
Rufus Brevett
Matthew Rose
Wayne Fereday
Tony Thorpe
Michael Meaker
Kevin Gallen

QPR 4–3 Chelsea (Meaker 3, Gallen)
QPR 4–4 Watford (Gallen 3, Meaker)

Final
QPR 2–3 Watford (Thorpe, Gallen)

BAD CAT

One of QPR's more bizarre red cards came in the 2–1 defeat to Preston in February 2005. Referee Lee Probert decided to give Rangers' 7ft mascot Jude the Cat his marching orders after officials kept confusing him with the players. Of the sending off, Jude said at the time:

> I'm very upset. Nothing like this has ever happened before, how can I be mistaken for a player? I'm a 7ft black cat! We're waiting to hear from the FA. I might be banned from the touchline or have to change my kit. And if that's not bad enough, I've been told my smoked salmon and cream might be taken away. I'll be back on Kitekat and semi-skimmed milk. I'm also worried that someone might find out my real identity. Hardly anyone knows who Jude really is and I haven't even told my closest friends what I do on a Saturday. We're playing Wolves next week and their mascot, Wolfie, wants to know whether I'll be there or not. He's said if I'm banned he'll stay away – he'll go on strike.

Luckily for Jude, no further action was taken and the feline was allowed back on the Rangers touchline the following week.

LOFTUS ROAD LEGEND – LES FERDINAND

Les' career began in non-league football with first Southall and then Hayes. His impressive strike rate at that level caught the attention of QPR and Rangers signed the striker for £15,000 in 1986. He was still a player with raw potential but Jim Smith could see a star in him and sent him on loan first to Brentford and then Turkish side Besiktas to gain some first-team experience. His time in Turkey was successful, with his 21 goals that season helping the side to a league and cup double. Back at Loftus Road, Trevor Francis was now in charge and Les struggled to break into the team. Indeed, he was about to leave the club until Don Howe replaced Francis in December 1989.

Under Howe, Les scored his first Rangers goals in a 4–2 victory over Chelsea and over the next two seasons formed a profitable partnership with Roy Wegerle – including memorable strikes against Luton Town and in the famous 3–1 win at Anfield over Liverpool.

Howe was soon replaced by Gerry Francis and under his stewardship Ferdinand emerged as a truly great front man. In 1992/93, Les' goals led Rangers to their best top-flight finish since the 1984, as they claimed fifth place. He finished the season with 20 goals, just 2 behind the league's top scorer Teddy Sheringham. His efforts were rewarded with an England call-up – he scored on his international debut against San Marino and would go on to earn 17 caps.

Over the next two seasons Ferdinand would again top the Rs' goalscoring charts and become a true QPR legend, earning the nickname Sir Les. The big boys soon started showing an interest in him and in the summer of 1995 Newcastle fought off competition from Arsenal among others to sign Les for a club record sale of £6 million. That following campaign Rangers struggled without their talisman and the money received from his sale was wasted by Ray Wilkins on the likes of Ned Zelic and Simon Osborn, resulting in relegation. Les, on the other hand, having moved to the North-East, flourished in the Newcastle side that finished second and was voted the PFA Player of the Year. After Newcastle Les joined Spurs but injuries were beginning to take their toll and he never really found his best form again, despite scoring the landmark 10,000th Premier League goal.

He spent six seasons at White Hart Lane before enjoying spells with West Ham, Leicester and Bolton, and ended his career with Reading where he scored once in 12 appearances. Now Les splits his time between coaching strikers at Tottenham and appearing on various TV channels as a pundit.

DID YOU KNOW?

On Les' debut for Besiktas, the club's fans allegedly sacrificed a sheep in the striker's honour.

WARTIME RANGERS

Football took a hiatus in September 1939, following Germany's attack on Poland and war breaking out in Europe. Young players were called into service to fight and with no games, teams had no way to generate money and professional players suddenly found themselves unemployed. Instead, the clubs tried to arrange friendlies and QPR took part in the very first wartime game, when they played an Army XI at Loftus Road on 9 September 1939.

After the initial stop, the FA decided to organise a new league system to keep clubs afloat during the war and on 21 October Rangers played their first game in the newly formed League South B. The league consisted of five teams from the London area along with Portsmouth, Southampton, Bournemouth, Brighton & Hove Albion and Reading. It proved to be a successful season for Rangers as they finished top of the League South, 2 points clear of Bournemouth. The club's only other success during this period came in 1943 when Rangers reached the League Cup South final, only to lose to Arsenal 4–1.

With clubs deprived of several regular players during this time, the FA allowed teams to loan players from other teams when needed to fulfil a fixture. Thus it became customary for players to guest for other teams and 'guest players' were frequently used by QPR, and likewise many of Rangers' players guested for a number of different clubs, especially those around London. Most notable was Billy McEwan, who between 1940 and 1944 guested for no fewer than seven clubs including going as far as Birmingham and Blackpool. The total number of guest appearances by QPR players in each season was:

1939/40	15 different players played a total of 73 guest appearances and scored 10 goals
1940/41	7 players made 16 guest appearances, 2 goals
1941/42	8 players made 35 guest appearances, 2 goals
1942/43	12 players made 60 guest appearances, 3 goals
1943/44	8 players made 26 guest appearances, 4 goals
1944/45	8 players made 30 guest appearances, 0 goals
1945/46	3 players made 18 guest appearances, 11 goals

QPR sadly lost three former players during the Second World War: Albert Bonass was killed in August 1945 when a Stirling bomber crashed on a training flight; Charlie Clark, who played six times for Rangers between 1936 and 1938; and Alan Fowler who guested for QPR during the 1940/41 season but lost his life in August 1944.

CAN'T BE TOO CAREFUL . . .

QPR were forced to postpone a First Division game with Sheffield United in September 1999 when Hungarian midfielder George Kulcsar contracted meningitis. Rangers closed their Loftus Road stadium and training ground in Acton, sent players home and put them on red alert for symptoms. Gavin Peacock, Karl Ready and Matthew Rose were also closely monitored having been taken ill at the same time, but it was Kulcsar who suffered most with a viral strain of the disease. Thankfully he made a full recovery and returned to the first team later that year.

WILD THING

Off the pitch, Gareth Ainsworth was just as entertaining as he was on it. As lead singer of rock band Dog Chewed The Handle, which released an album in 2008, he regularly toured the local pubs in West London. This led to the winger's trademark celebration of a guitar strum and the nickname 'Wild Thing'.

SINKING FUND

On Saturday 4 May 1912, Rangers, the reigning Southern League champions, played Blackburn Rovers in season curtain-raiser the Charity Shield at White Hart Lane. The match ended in a 2–1 win for Blackburn Rovers and all the proceeds from the game, some £265 10s 11d were donated to the *Titanic* Disaster Fund, with it being just three weeks after the ship had sunk in the Atlantic Ocean.

PREMIER Rs

QPR were founding members of the Premier League upon its inauguration in 1992 and competed in the first four seasons of the league, before their relegation in 1996. Here are some stats and facts on Rangers' first Premier League era.

Rangers' first Premier League game was away at Manchester City on Monday 17 August 1992. The game finished 1–1 with Andy Sinton cancelling out David White's opener. Three days later, QPR hosted Southampton in their first home game with goals from David Bardsley and a brace from Les Ferdinand giving the club a 3–1 win.

Rangers finished fifth in the in the debut Premier League season, their highest position since 1984 and making them the top London club.

Les Ferdinand finished the 1992/93 season with 20 goals, just 2 behind the league's top scorer Teddy Sheringham.

On Easter weekend 1993, Rangers recorded back-to-back wins over Nottingham Forest and Everton – scoring 9 goals in the process. The 4–3 win over Forest and 5–3 victory at Goodison Park also included back-to-back hat-tricks for Les Ferdinand.

Rangers' biggest win of the era was 5–1 over Coventry City in 1993. Bradley Allen (2), Les Ferdinand, Andy Impey and Simon Barker were on the scoresheet and the result prompted the resignation of City manager Bobby Gould after the game.

QPR lost 4–0 on 4 separate occasions during the last Premier League years, their biggest defeats during those 4 years. The games were West Ham (A) in August 1993, Leeds United (H) in April 1994, Blackburn Rovers (A) in November United 1994 and Leeds United (A) in January 1995.

Andy Impey made more appearances than any other QPR player during the last Premier League era, with 138. He was closely followed by David Bardsley (130), Simon Barker (126), Clive Wilson (119) and Alan McDonald (115).

Unsurprisingly it was Les Ferdinand who scored the most goals, netting 60 strikes in 108 appearances between 1992/93 and 1995/96.

After finishing fifth in 1992/93, Rangers other placings were ninth (1993/94), eighth (1994/95) and nineteenth (1995/96).

Taking into account all Premier League results from 1992/93 and up to and including the 2010/11 season, QPR would find themselves twenty-ninth in the all-time Premier League table.

Pos	Team	Years	P	W	D	L	F	A	GD	Pts
1	Man Utd	19	734	472	158	104	1,452	627	825	1,574
2	Arsenal	19	734	394	197	143	1,271	668	603	1,379
3	Chelsea	19	734	383	189	162	1,217	695	522	1,338
4	Liverpool	19	734	366	184	184	1,189	713	476	1,282
5	Aston Villa	19	734	276	223	235	936	870	66	1,051
6	Tottenham	19	734	274	195	265	1,006	979	27	1,017
7	Everton	19	734	257	207	270	924	939	-15	978
8	Newcastle	17	654	258	178	218	940	834	106	952
9	Blackburn	17	658	254	177	227	879	829	50	939
10	West Ham	16	616	202	158	256	723	880	-157	764
11	Man City	14	544	183	146	215	678	707	-29	695
12	Leeds	12	468	189	125	154	641	573	68	692
13	M'boro	14	568	160	156	220	621	741	-120	633[*]
14	Soton	13	506	150	137	219	598	738	-140	587
15	Bolton	12	456	139	122	195	529	668	-139	539
16	Fulham	10	380	116	111	153	432	501	-69	459
17	Coventry	9	354	99	112	143	387	490	-103	409
18	Sunderland	10	380	101	92	187	377	560	-183	395
19	Sheff Wed	8	316	101	89	126	409	453	-44	392
20	Wimbledon	8	316	99	94	123	384	472	-88	391
21	Charlton	8	304	93	82	129	342	442	-100	361
22	Leicester	8	308	84	90	134	354	456	-102	342
23	Birmingham	7	266	73	82	11	273	360	-87	301
24	Portsmouth	7	266	79	65	122	292	380	-88	293[**]

[*] Middlesbrough deducted 9 points for failing to fulfil a fixture in 1996.
[**] Portsmouth deducted 9 points for entering administration in 2010.

(table continued overleaf)

Pos	Team	Years	P	W	D	L	F	A	GD	Pts
25	Derby	7	266	68	70	128	271	420	-149	274
26	Wigan	6	228	65	57	106	227	347	-120	252
27	Nott'm F	5	198	60	59	79	229	287	-58	239
28	Ipswich	5	202	57	53	92	219	312	-93	224
29	QPR	4	164	59	39	66	224	232	-8	216
30	Norwich	4	164	50	51	63	205	257	-52	201
31	West Brom	5	190	39	52	99	188	322	-134	169
32	C Palace	4	160	37	49	74	160	243	-83	160
33	Stoke	3	114	36	30	48	118	151	-33	138
34	Sheff Utd	3	122	32	36	54	128	168	-40	132
35	Wolves	3	114	27	30	57	116	199	-83	111
36	Reading	2	76	26	13	37	93	113	-20	91
37	Oldham	2	84	22	23	39	105	142	-37	89
38	Hull City	2	76	14	23	39	73	139	-66	65
39	Bradford	2	76	14	20	42	68	138	-70	62
40	Watford	2	76	11	19	46	64	136	-72	52
41	Blackpool	1	38	10	9	19	55	78	-23	39
42	Barnsley	1	38	10	5	23	37	82	-45	35
43	Burnley	1	38	8	6	24	42	82	-40	30
44	Swindon	1	42	5	15	22	47	100	-53	30

STAR RELATIVE

Billy Cotton, a QPR director during the 1960s and presenter of popular BBC radio show *The Billy Cotton Band Show*, was the great-great-uncle of current TV and radio personality Fearne Cotton.

GOALFESTS

Rangers' record win was on 3 December 1960 when the Rs beat Tranmere Rovers 9–2 in a Third Division game. However, they've also been involved in some other memorable high-scoring affairs. Here are the best of Rangers' goalfests:

QPR 5–5 Newcastle United
22 September 1984, Division One

An incredible game in which QPR found themselves 4–0 down at half time thanks to a majestic first half performance from England international Chris Waddle. It took just 3 minutes for the winger to break the Rangers defence, when his run and cross set up Neil McDonald for an easy far-post header. Then, in 24 sparkling minutes Waddle looked to have killed off the game with the first hat-trick of his career. He slipped the first under Peter Hucker after 17 minutes, drilled a second off a Kenny Wharton rebound and curved a 25-yard strike beyond Hucker 4 minutes from the interval. QPR boss Alan Mullery told his team at the break that, 'There is no way you can score 4 goals,' but 2 minutes into the second period his team began a mission to prove their manager wrong when Gary Bannister headed home off Kevin Carr's parried shot. It was now Rangers who were in the driving seat and Simon Stainrod's 54th-minute strike put the Rs right back in the game. John Gregory then reduced the gap to one goal with a glorious lob from Micklewhite's pass with a quarter of the game left to play. Newcastle interrupted QPR's celebrations when Waddle once again set up Wharton to tap in United's fifth in what looked like the clinching goal. However, within 60 seconds Steve Wicks headed in a Micklewhite cross to bring the score to 5–4. Micklewhite then conjured up the game's remarkable punchline, slipping onto an Ian Stewart pass and rifling a shot into the roof of the net in injury time.

QPR team: Hucker, Neil, Dawes, Fereday, Wicks, Fenwick, Micklewhite, Fillery, Bannister, Stainrod, Gregory

QPR 6–0 Chelsea
31 March 1986, Division One

Rangers' greatest ever win over their West London rivals came on a windy Easter Monday on QPR's famous plastic pitch. Going into the match Chelsea were still in the mix for the league title but it was QPR who started the brighter and took the lead after just 8 minutes. John Byrne's initial shot was charged down but Gary Bannister followed up to drill into the bottom right-hand corner from an acute angle in front of the School End. Rangers doubled their advantage on 25 minutes. Byrne was involved again with a right wing cross, Terry Fenwick nodded the ball on and Bannister arrived in the 6-yard box to head home. A minute before the break, John Byrne picked up possession just inside the Chelsea half and dribbled past four startled defenders before letting fly from just inside the box. The fourth came on 58 minutes when Bannister tore away from the Chelsea back line and sent a low, bullet-like shot into the right-hand corner to complete a memorable treble for the striker. Byrne netted his second and Rangers' fifth on 68 minutes with a crisp finish before substitute Leroy Rosenior completed the rout running from the half way line and slipping the ball under Steve Francis.

QPR team: Barron, McDonald, Dawes, Fereday, Wicks, Fenwick (Rosenior), Allen, James, Byrne, Bannister, Robinson

Port Vale 4–4 QPR
January 1997, Division One

Thirteen years after the 5–5 draw with Newcastle, Rangers once again found themselves on the end of a first half 4-goal salvo, this time inflicted by Port Vale. Dean Glover opened the scoring for Vale, steering home from Jan Jansson's 24th-minute corner. The home side doubled their lead 10 minutes later when Steve Guppy's cross from the left was headed in at the far post by Lee Mills. Further goals from Ian Naylor and a Matthew Brazier own goal meant it looked all over for Rangers with only half of the game gone, but they were given a glimmer of hope when Vale debutant Jermaine Holwyn scored the second own goal of the afternoon in the 66th minute. And the visitors earned an incredible point with three goals in the last 5 minutes, beginning with an outstanding volley by substitute Andy Impey. Paul Murray then chipped a third 2 minutes from time and John Spencer crashed home an injury-time equaliser after Paul Musselwhite had beaten out an effort from substitute Daniele Dichio, sending the travelling Rangers fans into delirium.

QPR team: Roberts, Graham (Maddix), Brevett, Murray, McDonald, Ready, Spencer, Peacock, Hateley (Dichio), Brazier (Impey), Sinclair

QPR 6–0 Crystal Palace
9 May 1999, Division One
Going into this game, Rangers knew that only a win would be good enough to stop relegation to Division Two, as they welcomed South London rivals Crystal Palace to Loftus Road on the last day of the campaign. Rangers were on a run of five successive defeats but on 8 minutes George Kulcsar calmed their nerves, finishing off a clever move with a thumping volley that sailed past Kevin Miller in the Eagles' goal. The goal settled Rangers and they extended their lead 2 minutes before the break when Chris Kiwomya got on the end of huge Ludek Miklosko clearance to stab home at the second attempt. The QPR onslaught continued into the second half, and they made it 3–0 in the 56th minute when a Tony Scully free kick was flicked on by Steve Slade for Kiwomya to scramble in his second. Scully then got on the scoresheet himself with an unstoppable drive into the left-hand corner. The afternoon then got even worse for Palace as they were reduced to nine men following red cards to Fan Zhiyi and David Woozley. From the resulting penalty Tim Breacker made it 5, netting the rebound after Kiwomya missed the spot-kick. Kiwomya completed the rout with his hat-trick and Rangers' sixth when the striker beat Miller at the third attempt from close range. The win secured Rangers' First Division status amid jubilant scenes at Loftus Road.

QPR team: Miklosko, Breacker, Baraclough, Kulcsar, Linighan, Maddix, Scully, Peacock, Rowland (Murray), Slade, Kiwomya (Gallen)

MERRY CHRISTMAS

Up until the late 1950s Football League games were regularly played on Christmas Day. QPR played their first festive day game in 1900 and continued to compete on 25 December until the 1956/57 season when the fixture began to be phased out before being eventually removed in 1959. This is a complete record of all Rangers' Christmas Day results:

1900	Southern League Division One	QPR 2–0 Thames Ironworks (Bedingfield 2)
1907	Southern League Division One	QPR 0–0 Plymouth Argyle
1908	Southern League Division One	QPR 2–2 Norwich City (Rogers, Downing)
1909	Southern League Division One	QPR 1–0 Norwich City (Wilson)
1911	Southern League Division One	QPR 3–2 Crystal Palace (Thornton 2, Revill)
1912	Southern League Division One	QPR 1–0 Southampton (Birch)
1913	Southern League Division One	QPR 1–1 Norwich City (Birch)
1914	Southern League Division One	Bristol Rovers 1–3 QPR (Birch 2, Miller)
1915	London Combination	Watford 5–1 QPR (Humphries)
1916	London Combination	QPR 2–3 Arsenal (Dale, Hassan)

1917	London Combination	Brentford 1–1 QPR (Walters)
1918	London Combination	QPR 1–1 Tottenham Hotspur (Mitchell)
1919	Southern League Division One	QPR 2–0 Brentford (Mitchell, Broster)
1920	Division Three South	Brentford 0–2 QPR (Wilson 2)
1922	Division Three South	QPR 4–0 Luton Town (Parker 2, Birch 2)
1923	Division Three South	QPR 0–0 Charlton
1924	Division Three South	QPR 1–2 Norwich City (Ogley)
1925	Division Three South	QPR 2–2 Charlton Athletic (Burgess, Brown)
1926	Division Three South	QPR 2–4 Watford (Young, Mustard)
1928	Division Three South	QPR 4–2 Swindon Town (Rogers, Burns, Goddard, Kellard)
1929	Division Three South	Norwich City 3–0 QPR
1930	Division Three South	QPR 4–1 Notts County (Burns 3, Goddard)
1931	Division Three South	Torquay United 2–3 QPR (Collins 2, Cribb)

1933	Division Three South	QPR 2–0 Clapham Orient (Blackman, Brown)
1934	Division Three South	QPR 6–3 Clapham Orient (Blackman 2, Emmerson, Crawford, Devine, Allen)
1935	Division Three South	QPR 3–1 Watford (Cheetham 2, Ballantyne)
1936	Division Three South	QPR 4–0 Exeter City (Bott, Fitzgerald, Cheetham, Charlton)
1937	Division Three South	QPR 1–0 Southend United (Fitzgerald)
1939	League South	Fulham 3–8 QPR (Mangnall 3, Mallett 3, McCarthy, Bonass)
1940	League South	Brentford 2–1 QPR (Mangnall)
1941	League South	QPR 1–3 Crystal Palace (Harris)
1942	League South	QPR 2–1 Fulham (Mangnall, Sibley)
1943	League South	Brentford 2–5 QPR (Somerfield 2, Heathcote 2, Lowes)
1944	League South	Tottenham Hotspur 4–2 QPR (Abel, Lowes)

1945	Division Three South (North Region)	Norwich City 1–1 QPR (Ridyard)
1946	Division Three South	QPR 1–3 Ipswich Town (Hatton)
1948	Division Two	Blackburn Rovers 2–0 QPR
1950	Division Two	Preston North End 4–1 QPR (Waugh)
1951	Division Two	Barnsley 3–1 QPR (Hatton)
1953	Division Three South	Colchester United 5–0 QPR
1954	Division Three South	QPR 1–0 Northampton (Clark)
1956	Division Three South	Crystal Palace 2–1 QPR (Peacock)
1957	Division Three South	Gillingham 1–1 QPR (Standley)

Christmas day record:
P 44   W 21   D 9   L 14   F 85   A 74   Pts 50
(2 points for a win)

INDIAN SUMMER

After being enlisted into the RAF as a physical trainer during the Second World War, QPR front man Ivor Powell was posted to India and played for the RAF team alongside Rangers team-mate Billy McEwan. For each of their games two battalions of Indian troops were posted in the hills around the pitch to prevent local tribesmen getting within shooting distance of the spectators and players. In all Ivor and the players travelled 29,000 miles and played 126 games in 196 days while serving in India, often playing in the stifling heat and even against some local teams that played barefoot.

THE RIVALS

Traditionally QPR have enjoyed local rivalry with three neighbouring sides – Brentford, Fulham and Chelsea. Recent meetings against the three have been sparse, with the trio often in different divisions but they enjoyed healthy rivalries dating as far back as the late 1800s and up until the 1980s. They also contested in mini London Leagues during the wars, often playing each other up to four times a season.

Fulham

Rangers' rivalry with Fulham dates back the furthest (back before Chelsea were even founded), when the two teams met at Kensal Rise to contest the 1893 West London Observer Football Challenge Cup – which the Rs won 3–2. The win sparked an era that would see the two sides compete for the cup along with the West London League. Rangers' biggest win over the Cottagers was in 1939, when they thrashed Fulham 8–3 in a London South match – although this was at the outbreak of the Second World War when both teams had many players absent. The last meeting between the pair was in the 2000/01 season with Fulham running out 2–0 winners in a Division One match. Incredibly the 2011/12 season will mark the first ever top-flight meeting between the pair, having met in every other tier in English football.

Competition	P	W	D	L	F	A
Division Two	14	7	3	4	17	12
Division Three	8	5	1	2	12	10
FA Cup	8	2	2	4	14	10
League Cup	1	0	0	1	0	2
Southern Professional Floodlight Cup	1	0	0	1	0	2
Southern League	8	2	3	3	9	11
First World War League	14	3	2	9	12	25
Second World War League	13	3	5	5	35	37
Second World War Cup	2	0	0	2	6	11
Total	69	22	16	31	105	122

Chelsea

Despite being members of the Football League since 1920, QPR and neighbours Chelsea didn't meet in a competitive match until the 1968/69 season when Rangers made their First Division debut. Chelsea got the upper hand that day winning 4–0, but the pair would go on to enjoy a close rivalry over the next two decades competing for all the major honours. The most famous QPR win was on Easter Monday 1986, as Rangers all but ended Chelsea's title bid with a 6–0 thrashing of their West London neighbours. Throughout the 1980s the clubs failed to meet in any competition only twice, the 1983/84 season and the 1988/89 campaign. During the Premier League era, Rangers only managed one win over the Blues and since the Rs' relegation in 1996 the clubs have enjoyed contrasting fortunes, with Roman Abramovich's investment transforming the Kings Road outfit. More recently, other than a memorable pre-season victory in 2001 for Rangers, the sides' only meetings had come in two FA Cup games, both of which Chelsea won 1–0. The 2011/12 season marked the first time QPR, Fulham and Chelsea had appeared in the top flight together. In their Premier League clash at Loftus Road in October 2011, Heidar Helguson's penalty was enough to secure a 1–0 victory as Chelsea had two men sent off.

Competition	P	W	D	L	F	A
Division One	32	8	13	11	43	43
Division Two	8	3	2	3	10	9
FA Cup	5	1	1	3	4	7
League Cup	2	1	1	0	3	1
First World War League	16	3	2	11	14	35
First World War Cup	1	0	0	1	0	2
Second World War League	10	4	2	4	19	26
Second World War Cup	4	4	0	0	14	6
Total	78	24	21	33	107	129

Brentford

Brentford and QPR regularly competed with each other in local league and cup competitions during the early 1900s and became members of the Third Division South upon inclusion into the Football League in 1920. The sides enjoyed a close relationship over the next few decades, enjoying a period of 20 years between 1946 and 1966 that saw them meet in every season. The following campaign, however, saw contrasting fortunes for the clubs as Rangers were promoted and Brentford relegated, beginning a period that wouldn't see a match between the two until December 2002. Rangers got the better of the results that season, with Marc Bircham memorably scoring a 90th-minute winner in the game at Griffin Park. The last meeting was in February 2004, ending in a 1–1 draw.

Competition	P	W	D	L	F	A
Division Two	8	4	3	1	15	7
Division Three	54	17	19	18	70	81
FA Cup	4	0	1	3	3	8
Southern League	26	15	8	3	44	21
First World War League	16	3	6	7	18	38
Second World War League	11	5	1	5	29	21
Second World War Cup	6	2	1	3	7	8
Total	125	46	39	40	186	164

WEST LONDONERS

The following are players who have represented both QPR and one of their West London rivals.

QPR and Chelsea

Les Allen	Chelsea 1954–9	QPR 1965–71
Sylvan Anderton	Chelsea 1959–62	QPR 1962
Roy Bentley	Chelsea 1948–56	QPR 1961–2
James Bradshaw	Chelsea 1909–10	QPR 1910–11
Barry Bridges	Chelsea 1958–66	QPR 1968–70
Billy Brown	QPR 1910–11	Chelsea 1911–13
Gary Chivers	Chelsea 1978–83	QPR 1984–7
John Crawford	Chelsea 1923–4	QPR 1934–5
Mike Fillery	Chelsea 1978–82	QPR 1983–6
Allan Harris	Chelsea 1966–7	QPR 1967–71
John Hollins	Chelsea 1963–75	QPR 1975–9
Mark Falco	Chelsea 1982 (loan)	QPR 1988–91
Paul Furlong	Chelsea 1994–6	QPR 2000 (loan), 2002–7
Derek Gibbs	Chelsea 1955–60	QPR 1963–5
Vinnie Jones	Chelsea 1991–2	QPR 1998–9
Leon Knight	Chelsea 1999–2003	QPR 2001 (loan)
Tommy Langley	Chelsea 1974–80	QPR 1980–1
Frank Lyon	QPR 1903–7	Chelsea 1907–8
Andy Malcolm	Chelsea 1962	QPR 1962–5
Alan Mayes	QPR 1971–4	Chelsea 1980–3
Michael Mancienne	Chelsea 2006–11	QPR 2006–8 (loan)
John Mortimer	Chelsea 1956–65	QPR 1965–6
Brian Nicholas	QPR 1950–5	Chelsea 1955–7
Gavin Peacock	QPR 1984–7 & 1996–2	Chelsea 1993–6
John O'Rourke	Chelsea 1962–3	QPR 1971–3
Gilbert Overs	Chelsea 1910–11	QPR 1911–13
Steve Perkins	Chelsea 1971–7	QPR 1977–8
Michael Pinner	QPR 1959–60	Chelsea 1961–2
Derek Richardson	Chelsea 1974–6	QPR 1976–9

Ben Sahar	Chelsea 2006–9	QPR 2007 (loan)
Arthur Sales	Chelsea 1924–30	QPR 1920
Scott Sinclair	Chelsea 2005–10	QPR 2007 (loan)
Eddie Smith	Chelsea 1946–52	QPR 1957–8
Jimmy Smith	Chelsea 2005–9	QPR 2006–7 (loan)
Nigel Spackman	Chelsea 1983–7	QPR 1989
John Spencer	Chelsea 1992–7	QPR 1996–8
Joseph Spottiswoode	Chelsea 1919–20	QPR 1925
Bill Steer	QPR 1909–11	Chelsea 1911
Mark Stein	QPR 1988–9	Chelsea 1993–8
Terry Venables	Chelsea 1960–6	QPR 1969–74
Ian Watson	Chelsea 1960–5	QPR 1965–73
Clive Walker	Chelsea 1976–84	QPR 1986–7
Dave Webb	Chelsea 1968–74	QPR 1974–7
Roy Wegerle	Chelsea 1986–8	QPR 1990–2
Richard Whittaker	Chelsea 1952–60	QPR 1963–7
Steve Wicks	Chelsea 1974–8	QPR 1979–81
Alan Wilks	Chelsea 1963–5	QPR 1965–71
Ray Wilkins	Chelsea 1973–9	QPR 1989–94
Andy Wilson	Chelsea 1923–31	QPR 1931–2
Clive Wilson	Chelsea 1987–90	QPR 1990–5
Shaun Wright-Phillips	Chelsea 2005–8	QPR 2011–

QPR and Fulham

Charles Abel	Fulham 1931–3	QPR 1934
Ernest Adams	Fulham 1947	QPR 1947
Edward Anderson	Fulham 1904–5	QPR 1906
Dennis Bailey	Fulham 1986	QPR 1991–3
Ernest Beecham	Fulham 1923–32	QPR 1932–5
Roy Bentley	Fulham 1956–60	QPR 1960–2
Fred Bevan	QPR 1904	Fulham 1907
Albert Blake	Fulham 1928–9	QPR 1933–6
Matthew Brazier	QPR 1994–8	Fulham 1998–9
Rufus Brevett	QPR 1991–8	Fulham 1998–2003

Frank Cannon	QPR 1907–9	Fulham 1910
Dave Clement	QPR 1965–79	Fulham 1980–1
Dean Coney	Fulham 1980–7	QPR 1987–8
Lee Cook	QPR 2002–3 (loan), 2004–7 & 2008–	Fulham 2007–8
Lloyd Evans	QPR 1904–5	Fulham 1905–6
Joseph Fidler	Fulham 1905–6	QPR 1906–13
Bill Haley	Fulham 1928–31	QPR 1931–2
Robbie Herrera	QPR 1988–93	Fulham 1993–8
Ernie Howe	Fulham 1973–7	QPR 1977–82
Bobby Keetch	Fulham 1962–6	QPR 1966–8
Jim Langley	Fulham 1957–65	QPR 1965–7
Thomas Leigh	Fulham 1907–10	QPR 1910–11
Bill Mason	Fulham 1928–33	QPR 1933–9
Rodney Marsh	Fulham 1962–6 & 1976–7	QPR 1966–72
Hugh McQueen	QPR 1901–2	Fulham 1902–3
David Metchick	Fulham 1961–4	QPR 1968–70
Peter Molloy	Fulham 1931–3	QPR 1935–6
Dave Nelson	Fulham 1946–7	QPR 1949–51
Paul Parker	Fulham 1982–7	QPR 1987–91
Paul Peschisolido	Fulham 1997–2001	QPR 2000 (loan)
Zesh Rehman	Fulham 2004–6	QPR 2006–9
Leroy Rosenior	Fulham 1982–5	QPR 1985–7
Barry Salvage	Fulham 1967–9	QPR 1970–3
Tony Sealy	QPR 1981–3	Fulham 1983–5
Ernest Shepherd	Fulham 1938–48	QPR 1950–7
Tommy Simmons	Fulham 1914	QPR 1914–18
Ernie Symes	Fulham 1917–23	QPR 1924
Jim Taylor	Fulham 1945–52	QPR 1952–4
Richard Teale	QPR 1974–5	Fulham 1976–7
Dave Underwood	QPR 1949–52	QPR 1963–5
Clive Walker	QPR 1986–7	Fulham 1987–90
Callum Willock	Fulham 2000–3	QPR 2000 (loan)
Christer Warren	Fulham 1997 (loan)	QPR 2000–2
Arthur Wood	Fulham 1911–18	QPR 1923

QPR and Brentford

Brian Bedford	QPR 1959–65	Brentford 1966–7
Marcus Bean	QPR 2002–6	Brentford 2008–
Marcus Bent	Brentford 1995–8	QPR 2010 (loan)
Mark Benstead	QPR 1981–5	Brentford 1990
Stan Bowles	QPR 1972–9	Brentford 1981
Steve Burke	QPR 1979–86	Brentford 1986 (loan)
Gary Cooper	QPR 1983–6	Brentford 1985 (loan)
William Cross	QPR 1904–5	Brentford 1905
Fred Durrant	Brentford 1939–46	QPR 1946–9
Lloyd Evans	QPR 1904–5	Brentford 1907–8
Les Ferdinand	QPR 1987–95	Brentford 1988 (loan)
Mark Fleming	QPR 1987–89	Brentford 1989–91
George Francis	Brentford 1953–61	QPR 1961
Allan Glover	QPR 1968–9	Brentford 1976–7
James Langley	Brentford 1946–9	QPR 1965–9
Mark Lazarus	QPR 1960–1, 1961–2 & 1966–8	Brentford 1964–6
Gavin Mahon	Brentford 1998–2002	QPR 2008–11
Billy McAdams	Brentford 1962–5	QPR 1964–6
Thomas McGovern	Brentford 1918–20	QPR 1920–4
Thomas McKenzie	QPR 1908	Brentford 1908
George McLeod	Brentford 1958–64	QPR 1964–5
Archibald Mitchell	QPR 1907–21	QPR 1921
Sam Morris	QPR 1908–11	Brentford 1920
Dave Nelson	Brentford 1947–50	QPR 1949–51
Mick O'Brien	Brentford 1919–20	QPR 1920–2
Johnny Pearson	Brentford 1955–7	QPR 1958–60
Edward Pince	Brentford 1912–20	QPR 1920

Bill Pointon	QPR 1948–50	Brentford 1950–1
Keith Pritchett	QPR 1974–5	Brentford 1976–7
Martin Rowlands	Brentford 1998–3	QPR 2003–
Harold Salt	QPR 1926–7	Brentford 1929–32
Barry Salvage	QPR 1970–3	Brentford 1973–5
Kenny Sansom	QPR 1989–91	Brentford 1993
Tony Sealy	QPR 1981–3	Brentford 1991
Thomas Shufflebottom	Brentford 1902–3	QPR 1904–6
Barry Silkman	Brentford 1980	QPR 1980–1
Tommy Simmons	Brentford 1913–14	QPR 1914–18
Andy Sinton	Brentford 1985–9	QPR 1989–93
Steve Slade	QPR 1996–2000	Brentford 2007 (loan)
George Smith	Brentford 1945–7	QPR 1947–9
George Stewart	Brentford 1946–7	QPR 1947–53
Ian Stewart	QPR 1980–3	Brentford 1988 (loan)
Sidney Sugden	QPR 1905–8	Brentford 1908–9
Jim Towers	Brentford 1954–62	QPR 1961–2
Rowan Vine	Brentford 2002–3 (loan) & 2010–11 (loan)	QPR 2007–
Herbert Young	Brentford 1925–6	QPR 1929–30

PINT PLEASE

While using Latimer Road as their home ground between 1901 and 1904, the players had to contend with a site that had no changing rooms. Instead the players used to change in the nearby public house, The Latimer Arms, and walk down to the ground in their playing kit.

LONDON VENUE

Loftus Road hasn't just played host to football in its 94-year history – there have been a number of other events held at the West London venue as well. It has twice hosted international rugby games as part of the Gillette Tri-Nations Rugby League competition. The first, in 2004, saw Australia beat New Zealand 32–16 and was followed by Great Britain's 26–42 loss to the All Blacks a year later. Rugby games were also a familiar sight at the ground in the mid-1950s, when international Rugby Union games were a regular occurrence.

Away from ball sports, Barry McGuigan successfully challenged Eusebio Pedroza to become WBA World Featherweight Champion at a bout held at Loftus Road in 1985 and the ground even hosted a rock concert in May 1975 when Yes performed at the stadium.

FIVE GREAT HAT-TRICKS

George Goddard v Merthyr Tydfil
1 December 1932, FA Cup
The occasion may have been a run-of-the-mill FA Cup game against Merthyr Tydfil, but the importance won't have been lost on Rangers striker George Goddard. His 3 goals in the team's 5–1 win was Goddard's 16th treble for the club, a record that still stands today. Merthyr must have been sick of the sight of Goddard as not only did his goals knock the side out of the cup that day, it was also the third hat-trick the QPR striker had scored against them in four seasons.

Stan Bowles v Brann Bergen
15 September 1976 & 29 September 1976, UEFA Cup
Rangers took to their first ever European campaign like a duck to water, and none more so than maverick Stanley Bowles. The

QPR number 10 scored hat-tricks in both the home and away legs of the competition's opening round against Brann Bergen, and would go on to score 11 in total in the season's UEFA Cup. He opened his European account in front of the Loftus Road crowd half an hour into the first leg, getting on the end of a Dave Webb flick-on. Bowles netted again 4 minutes later, with a low drive and then completed his hat-trick in the 64th minute. Not content with a first European treble, he repeated the feat a fortnight later, helping the Rs to a massive 7–0 aggregate victory in their first ever European tie.

Gary Bannister v Chelsea
31 March 1986, Division One
Before the recent Premier League win over Chelsea, Rangers' most famous West London victory came on Easter Monday 1986, with a 6-goal blitz that included a treble from Gary Bannister. It took him just 8 minutes to open the scoring; pouncing on John Byrne's charged-down shot to slot the ball home from the left-hand side of the box. On 25 minutes, Bannister doubled his tally as Byrne's cross was headed on by Terry Fenwick and the striker stooped in for his second. With the sun now shining on Loftus Road, Bannister completed his hat-trick on the hour, with a low drive across the goalkeeper and into the corner of the net.

Dennis Bailey v Manchester United
1 January 1992, Division One
Bailey ensured his name would forever be etched in Rangers folklore with a memorable hat-trick at Old Trafford on New Year's Day 1992. QPR were already 1–0 up when Bailey netted his first with just 5 minutes on the clock. Andy Sinton hooked the ball forward, and the Rangers number 9 fought off the challenge of Clayton Blackmore to stab the ball home. Into the second half and Bailey made it 3–0, chipping Peter Schmeichel after a neat little run on goal and his day was complete when he was on hand to tap the ball in from 3 yards when Sinton's shot hit the post for the memorable treble.

Les Ferdinand v Everton
12 April 1993, Premier League

Just 3 days before this fixture, Ferdinand had netted a hat-trick in a 4–3 win over Nottingham Forest, and added a second treble to his eventual 24-goal tally in a 5–3 win at Goodison Park. The first came on 38 minutes, when Andy Sinton teed up the England front-man on the edge of the box to drill home. His second came after the break, as Neville Southall made a mess of an Andy Impey cross and the ball fell for Ferdinand for an easy finish. Ferdinand then completed his hat-trick on 51 minutes by finishing off a neat one-two with Bradley Allen and smashing the ball into the back of the net.

HAT-TRICK FACTS

First: Peter Turnball v West Hampstead October 1899

Most: 16 – George Goddard 1927–32, 14 – Brian Bedford 1960–4

First top flight: Don Givens v Derby County February 1975

First European: Stan Bowles v Brann Bergen September 1976

First of the new millennium: Andy Thomson v Port Vale September 2001

Longest run between hat-tricks: 3 years and 332 days – Cureton 2004 to Ledesma 2008

Most hat-tricks in one season (team): 7 – 1929/30 and 1961/62

Most hat-tricks in one season (player): 6 – Brian Bedford 1961/62

QUICK OFF THE MARK

Tommy Langley's strike at home to Bolton Wanderers on 11 October 1980 holds the record for the fastest goal in QPR history, timed at just 10 seconds! The left-footed shot helped

Rangers to a 3–1 win over the Trotters in a Division Two fixture watched by 8,641 fans.

NUMBER 31

In 2007 Rangers made the difficult decision to retire the club's number 31 shirt in honour of striker Ray Jones. Jones, who wore the number for the majority of his short career, passed away in a tragic car accident on 25 August along with two others, aged just 18. His team-mates paid tribute to the young star by each wearing his name on the back of the shirts during a match with Southampton the following month, while fans still sing his name to this day. He made 37 appearances for the Rs, scoring 6 goals and will always be remembered fondly at Loftus Road.

5 STAR

The most goals scored by one player in one game was 5, when Alan Wilks netted all of Rangers' goals in a 5–1 win over Oxford United in October 1967.

93 AND OUT

Ivor Powell made over 100 appearances for Rangers in an 11-year spell that saw him become the club's first Welsh international. However, he also holds a place in the Guinness World Records as the world's oldest football coach, at the grand old age of 93. Powell's coaching career started at Port Vale in 1951, then he had spells at Bradford City, Carlisle United, PAOK and finally Bath City. He remained on the coaching staff at Bath for 30 years until his retirement in May 2010.

WORLD CUP R

The only World Cup winner to have appeared in a Rangers shirt is Argentina's Osvaldo 'Ossie' Ardiles. The 1978 winner played 8 games in a short spell during the 1988/89 season.

THE GOAL THAT NEVER WAS

One of the most bizarre goals ever scored at Loftus Road came in a Division One match between QPR and Blackburn Rovers on 13 November 1982. With the scores level at 1–1, Rovers launched an attack down the left-hand side towards the School End. The ball was crossed to the near post by David Hamilton and went harmlessly out of play for a goal kick, but in doing so caught the back stanchion holding up the net and rebounded back into play. Rovers' Norman Bell then nipped in and jokingly nipped the ball back into the net only for the referee to amazingly give that goal thinking that Peter Hucker had tipped the ball onto the bar and back into play.

Pandemonium ensued with all 9,000 people in the ground well aware the ball had gone out of play and QPR players incandescent with rage. The story then goes that John Gregory kicked the ball into the Ellerslie Road stand and told QPR fans to keep hold of it while they argued with the referee. Manager Terry Venables also made his way onto the field to speak with the officials. However, the goal stood and Rangers had to rely on a late Terry Fenwick penalty to rescue something from the game. Rangers immediately changed the design of the goals at the ground, removing the full-length back stanchions and replacing them with the smaller curved ones at the top of the posts.

LOFTUS ROAD LEGEND – KEVIN GALLEN

A product of the QPR youth system and Rs fan, Gallen scored an amazing 153 goals in 110 games for the Rangers youth team, breaking Jimmy Greaves' long-held record at that level. Gallen also memorably partnered Robbie Fowler in the impressive England U18 team that won the 1993 U18 European Championships which also included Paul Scholes and Sol Campbell. He was soon knocking on the Rangers first-team door and made his debut on the opening day of the 1994/95 season at Old Trafford in a 2–0 defeat to Manchester United before scoring on his first senior appearance at Loftus Road against Sheffield Wednesday three days later.

That year he formed an impressive partnership with Les Ferdinand scoring 10 goals in his first full season in the Premier League. That summer, however, Ferdinand was sold and the pressure on the team and young Gallen was too much, Rangers being relegated that season. Much was expected for the following campaign with Gallen leading Rangers' bid for an instant Premier League return, but disaster struck in the second game of the season against Portsmouth when Kevin injured his knee ligaments while scoring a goal in the 2–1 win. It was an injury that kept him out for almost a year and half and once he returned he struggled with form and fitness.

Upon his return to the side Gallen found himself down the pecking order for a place in the frontline and although there were some highlights, Rangers decided to let Gallen go in the summer of 2000 and he joined Huddersfield Town and later Barnsley. He never really settled in the North, and although he scored on his return to Loftus Road with the Terriers, he took a pay-cut to return home to QPR, now in Division Two and under Ian Holloway in November 2001.

Over the next 5 seasons he played a key part in Rangers' promotion back to the Championship, forming a lethal partnership with Paul Furlong and being named club captain. He finished his Rangers career in 2007 joining MK Dons as

QPR's sixth top scorer in their history and later played for Luton Town, Barnet and Braintree Town.

DID YOU KNOW?

Kevin Gallen is good mates with singer Morrissey, having met him on holiday in LA in 2005. Gallen even sent Morrissey a personalised kit with 'Mozalini 10' on the back that the former Smiths frontman has been pictured wearing on his website.

ACKNOWLEDGMENTS

I would like to thank the following people and publications for making this title and its contents possible. To Kevin Gallen, for his insights, stories of the club and for being kind enough to write the foreword for the title, and to Paul Finney and David Fraser for making it possible. To QPR historian Gordon Macey for his willingness, knowledge and publication *Queens Park Rangers: The Complete Record*; to Ian Taylor at QPR; publications including *The Little Book of QPR* by David Clayton; *The Sunderland AFC Miscellany* by Paul Days; *Gas Masks For Goal Posts* by Anton Rippon; *The QPR Quiz Book* by Chris Cowlin and Kevin Snelgrove; *Heroes in Hoops* by John Marks; *Soccer at War* by Jack Rollin; websites including indyrs.co.uk, Loftforwords, qprreport and qprnet and to Richard Leatherdale at the History Press for his encouragement.

I would also like to thank Ian Pollard for giving me my opportunity; to my Dad for taking me to Loftus Road for the first time in 1992 and to my Mum and all my family and friends for all their support; and finally to Jo for her love, endless supply of cheese sandwiches and constant belief in me.

Thank you also to QPR for providing so much material and wonderful memories. U RRRRS!